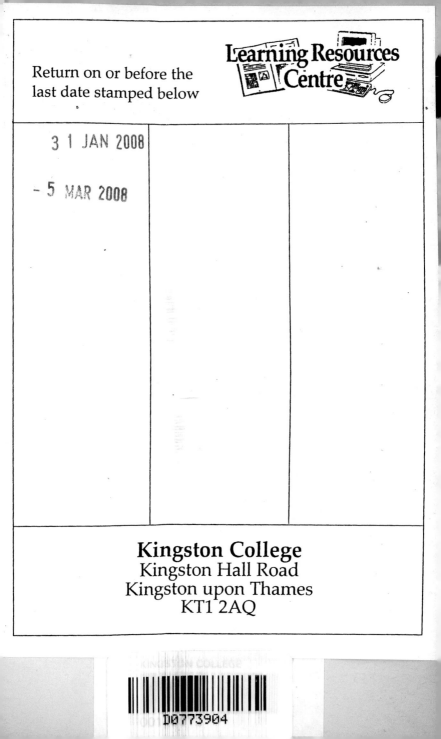

Published by Methuen 2005

1 3 5 7 9 10 8 6 4 2

First published in 2005 by
Methuen Publishing Limited
11–12 Buckingham Gate
London SW1E 6LB

Methuen Publishing Limited Reg. No. 3543167

A CIP catalogue record for this book is available from
the British Library

ISBN 0 413 77548 8

Typeset by Country Setting, Kingsdown, Kent
Printed and bound in Great Britain by
Bookmarque Ltd, Croydon, Surrey

THE CORN EXCHANGE PRESENTS

DUBLIN BY LAMPLIGHT

**BY MICHAEL WEST IN COLLABORATION WITH THE COMPANY
DIRECTED BY ANNIE RYAN**

CAST

Jimmy Finnegan	Mike Carbery
Eva St. John	Karen Egan
Willy Hayes	Louis Lovett
Frank Hayes	Fergal McElherron
Maggie	Janet Moran
Martyn Wallace	Mark O'Halloran

Music composed and performed by	Conor Linehan

Director	Annie Ryan
Set Design	Kris Stone
Costume Design	Sinéad Cuthbert

Based on an original lighting design by	Matt Frey
Tour Lighting	Rob Furey

Producer	Sarah Durcan
Production Manager	Des Kenny
Stage Director	Margarita Corscadden
Stage Manager	Lisa Mahony
Set Construction	Theatre Production Services
Scenic Artist	Sandra Butler
Photographer	Paul McCarthy
Graphic Design	Scott Burnett - Aad.
Marketing	Jennifer Jennings
Publicity	Emma Schad

TRAVERSE THEATRE, EDINBURGH August 2005
By arrangement with Richard Wakely

Dublin by Lamplight premiered in Project Arts Centre,
Dublin November 1st 2004.

THANK YOU:

The Arts Council, Culture Ireland, The Corn Exchange Board of
Directors, Philip Howard, Mike Griffiths, Laura Collier, Gavin Harding,
Andy Catlin, Renny Robertson, Martin Duffield, Shelia Mackie, Lee
Davies, Laura Jukes and all at Traverse; Len Abrahamson, Lorraine
Brennan, Siobhán Colgan, Ronan Conway, Jane Cox, Vincent Doherty,
Marie Donnelly, Ann Doyle, Frank and Toni Durcan, Tracey Elliston,
Julian Erskine, Halina Froudist, Seth Glewen, John Gribbin, Richard
Hilliard, Ken Hartnett, Wolfgang Hoffman, Ruth Hunter, Jennifer
Kingston, Jack Kirwan, Ruth Lehane, Eamon Little, Nicola McCutcheon
and Nick Seymour, Maureen McGlynn, Derick Mulvey, Tom Murphy,
Sinéad O'Doherty, Etáin O'Malley, Yvonne O'Reilly, Mickey Rolfe,
Pat and Dick Ryan, Oddie Sherwin, Jessica Thebus, Richard Wakely,
John and Cecily West, Trevor and Maura West; Willie White and Niamh
O'Donnell and all at Project, Linda McDonnell and the Leinster Cricket
Club, Marie Kearns at The Abbey, Don Shipley, Felicity O'Brien
and Ross Keane and all at Dublin Theatre Festival, Bea Kelleher and
Maedhbh McCullagh at the Dublin Fringe Festival, Polly O'Loughlin
and Matt Verso at the Pavilion, Tania Banotti and Amy O'Hanlon at
Theatre Forum, Christine Sisk at the Department of Arts, Sports and
Tourism, Cliona Maher at Audecon Consultants, Mark Dudgeon at
Methuen, Karl Toomey and Johnny Kelly at Aad.

Thank you also to those who do not wish to be credited.

WWW.CORNEXCHANGE.IE

Director's Note

In December 2003, we invited esteemed Chicago director and my good friend, Jessica Thebus, to explore what would happen if you combine our own strange take on Commedia dell'Arte with other ensemble techniques, in particular, Story Theatre. This is the work that myself and Jessica grew up doing in Chicago at the Piven Theatre Workshop, where an ensemble uses third person narration and groovy seventies theatre games to bring a story to life. With great satisfaction and relief, we found that when a Commedia character narrated his or her own action, it gave another dimension to the Commedia style, offering more potential for transformation. Equally, the intensity and energy of Commedia gave good old Story Theatre a sharp kick in the pants of its usual spooky, slow motion lyricism. It was a happy coupling.

In March 2004, we worked with six actors and Michael West to find our story. Michael wanted to do something around Dublin in 1904, the centenary year of the Abbey theatre and Joyce's setting for *Ulysses*. Our starting point for the story was Faust. But who would an Irish Faust be? Surely, if he could have anything he wanted, the first thing he would do would be to leave Ireland. Nevertheless, we were keen on staying in Dublin during that filthy time at the turn of the century. We played around with other Faust models, like Bulgakov's *The Master and Margarita*, as well as our favourite bits of Joyce and O'Casey, among other things. Something of Bulgakov's theatricals stayed, but the Devil went to hell and eventually this story of Dublin 1904 emerged.

Annie Ryan

Louis Lovett, Mike Carbery, Janet Moran and Mark O'Halloran in *Dublin by Lamplight*
© Paul McCarthy

About The Corn Exchange

In 1995 Annie Ryan spotted on the Dublin quays a crumbling Georgian façade with "The Corn Exchange" written on its rusting sign. "Corn" was the term used at New Crime, the Commedia dell'Arte troupe in her native Chicago, to describe a certain kind of theatre: theatre that would work its actors like dogs, but do anything for a cheap gag; theatre that would make its audience laugh and cry at the same time. It described a kind of wild irreverence within a strict and respected structure. It was the kernel of Commedia dell'Arte. It seemed the perfect name for a theatre company. The Corn Exchange was born.

If "Corn" described the flavour of the work, the "Exchange" element involved marrying this renegade version of Commedia dell'Arte from Chicago with other performance disciplines to see what happened. The common denominator for the work was an emphasis on the actor, the ensemble and experimentation.

The Corn Exchange has been creating dynamic, groundbreaking work in Ireland for ten years now. The company has presented adaptations of classics and new work in the style of Commedia dell'Arte, as well as new writing and site-specific work, and has toured Ireland, the UK and the US. The company continues to collaborate with internationally acclaimed theatre practitioners to explore the boundaries of theatre and what is possible within it.

Future work includes *Old People On Buses* (working title), an original devised piece from an idea by Mark O'Halloran for the Dublin Theatre Festival 2006, *Othello*, a reworking of the classic in the style of Commedia dell'Arte, and *Carmen*, an adaptation of the opera.

Simone Kirby and David Pearse in *Mud* © Paul McCarthy

Work to date:

Mud by María Irene Fornés
Winner Best Production Irish Times/ ESB Irish Theatre Awards 2003

Lolita by Nabokov, adapted by Michael West in partnership with The Abbey Theatre. Winner Best Costume Design, Best Actress Irish Times/ESB Irish Theatre Awards 2002

Foley by Michael West

Car Show original shows in cars by various writers
Winner Judges' Special Award Irish Times/ESB Irish Theatre Awards 1998 and the Cultural Inspiration Award

The Seagull by Anton Chekhov in a new adaptation by Michael West

A Play on Two Chairs by Michael West

Baby Jane by the company under the direction of Annie Ryan

Big Bad Woolf by the company under the direction of Annie Ryan
Nominated for two Irish Times/ESB Theatre Awards

Streetcar by the company under the direction of Annie Ryan
Winner of the Sexiest Show of the Dublin Fringe Festival 1996

Cultural Shrapnel a collection of performance pieces

Biographies

Annie Ryan
DIRECTOR

Originally from Chicago, Annie trained in acting and improvisation in the Piven Theatre Workshop and graduated from New York University's Tisch School of the Arts. She moved to Dublin in 1992 to work with Michael West. She founded The Corn Exchange for the first Dublin Fringe Festival in 1995 to explore different theatrical styles, in particular, the style of Commedia dell'Arte. Work with The Corn Exchange includes *Cultural Shrapnel, Streetcar, Big Bad Woolf, Baby Jane, A Play On Two Chairs, Car Show, The Seagull, Foley, Lolita* and *Mud*. She directed the children's show, *Rudolf the Red* for the Ark.

Michael West
WRITER

Michael West has worked extensively with The Corn Exchange, for whom he has also written *Foley*; the stage adaptation of *Lolita* (Abbey/Peacock); *A Play on Two Chairs*; a translation of *The Seagull*; and parts of *Car Show*. In collaboration with TEAM he has written two plays for children: *Forest Man* and *Jack Fell Down*. Other original plays include *Monkey, Snow, The Evidence of Things, The Gunpowder Plot* and *The Death of Naturalism*. He has also translated or adapted many texts, including *Stabat Mater Furiosa* by Jean-Pierre Siméon, *The Separation of Body and Soul* by Calderón, Molière's *Don Juan* and *The Marriage of Figaro* by Beaumarchais. His acclaimed translation of *Death and the Ploughman* for the Comédie de Reims, has been produced in London and most recently in New York in a production by SITI Theater Company, directed by Anne Bogart.

Kris Stone
SET DESIGNER

Kris Stone's designs have been seen throughout the United States and Europe in over 100 productions, earning her an Irish Theatre Award nomination for Best Set Design and the National Endowment for the Arts Award. Work with the Corn Exchange includes: *Lolita* (Abbey Theatre), and *Mud* (Project). Upcoming projects include: the opera *Brundibar* by Tony Kushner with Maurice Sendak, *The Real Thing* at Huntington Stage, *Private Lives* at Long Wharf Theatre, and a new Off-Broadway show *Cycling Past The Matterhorn* on 42nd Street. Kris studied at the Slade School of Fine Art in London, holds a BFA from the Art Institute of Chicago, and a MFA from The Yale School of Drama.

Conor Linehan
COMPOSER
Conor Linehan has worked extensively as a composer and pianist throughout Ireland and Britain. Theatre work includes: *Rebecca* (for David Pugh Ltd.) *The Cherry Orchard, She Stoops to Conquer, The Tempest, The Colleen Bawn, Love in the Title, Saint Joan, The Wake* (Abbey Theatre); *Peer Gynt, Playboy Of The Western World* (RNT), *Two Gentleman of Verona, Edward III, Loveplay, Luminosity* (RSC); *Rosencrantz and Guildenstern are Dead, Four Knights at Knaresborough* (West Yorkshire Playhouse) *The Mayor of Zalamea* (Liverpool Everyman), *Long Days Journey Into Night* (Gate Theatre) *Carthaginians, A Dolls House* (Lyric Belfast), *All's Well That Ends Well* (Classic Stage Ireland), *Antigone* (Storytellers) *Mermaids* (Coiscéim).

Matt Frey
LIGHTING DESIGNER
Matt Frey recently designed Harry Partch's opera *Oedipus* with Ridge Theater in New York. Also with Ridge: *Decasia* at St. Ann's Warehouse in Brooklyn and *The Death of Klinghoffer* at the BAM/Next Wave Festival. Designs include Melissa James Gibson's *Brooklyn Bridge* at The Children's Theatre Company in Minneapolis, Melissa James Gibson's plays *[sic]* and *Suitcase* at Soho Rep in New York, Neil Labute's new play *Fat Pig* for Manhattan Class Company. Other collaborations include *The Orphan of Zhao* (English version) conceived and directed by Chen Shi Zheng at the Lincoln Center Festival, Steve Reich and Beryl Korot's *Three Tales and The Cave* performed worldwide. Matt has also worked at Playwright's Horizons, New York Theatre Workshop, Signature Theater, Theatre For A New Audience, and regional theaters around the US.

Sinéad Cuthbert
COSTUME DESIGN
Born in Dublin, Sinéad's theatre designs include *King Lear* (Second Age) and *Rudolf the Red* (The Ark) *Chambermade* (Coiscéim), *Amadeus* (Ouroboros), *The Woman Who Walked Into Doors* (Up-Beat), *Hamlet* and *Macbeth* (Secondage and Theatreworks), *Tales From Ovid, Richard III* and *Mutabilitie* (Theatreworks – Winner Best Costume Designer Irish Times/ESB Awards 2000), *Midden* (Rough Magic), *Blush, Over The Rainbow, Bread and Circus* (Rex Levitates Dance Company) *Burn This* (Guna Nua) *Guess Who's Coming to Dinner* (Calypso) and *Pass The Parcel* (The Ark).

Mike Carbery
JIMMY FINNEGAN

Mike studied theatre and performance at Coláiste Dhúlaigh and Bull Alley respectively. Since graduating he has worked with such theatre companies as Barnstorm, Big Telly, Calypso, Corcadorca, Civic, The Corn Exchange, Kabosh, Macnas, Project, Reply, U-Man-Zoo and The Belgrade in Coventry. He has also danced in two productions for Rionach Ní Néill and has worked as a movement director on a children's theatre show for Barnstorm.

Karen Egan
EVA ST. JOHN

Acting credits include: *Smoke Me* (Pori Theatre Festival, Finland), *Just a Little One – A Dorothy Parker Cocktail* (Bewley's Café Theatre and on tour), her one-woman shows *Coalface Cabaret* (ESB Dublin Fringe Festival 2004) and *Café Cabaret* (Bewley's Café Theatre, The Helix and on tour), *The Odd Couple* (Civic Theatre and on tour), *Do Not Adjust Yourself* (Dublin Fringe Festival 2002 & Bewley's Café Theatre), *Car Show 3: Charlotte's Web* (The Corn Exchange). Film/TV includes: *Man About Dog* (Treasure Films), *Kiddo* (Perry Ogden), *A Man of No Importance, Wasted* (RTE), *Fair City* (RTE), *Liz and Margie – Live!* (RTE & LWT), *X-it File* (RTE) and *The Stand-Up Show* (BBC). Karen was a member of the comedy singing trio, *The Nualas*.

Louis Lovett
WILLY HAYES

Theatre work includes *Galileo* (Rough Magic Theatre Company), *The Whiteheaded Boy, God's Gift* and *The Temple of Clown* (Barabbas...the Company); *The Butterfly Ranch, Candide* and *The Seven Deadly Sins* (Performance Corporation); *She Stoops to Conquer* (Abbey Theatre); *Antigone* (Storytellers Theatre Company and Cork Opera House); *Who's afraid of Virgina Woolf* (Plush Theatre Productions); *Bumbógs and Bees* (TEAM) and *Diamonds in the Soil* (Macnas Theatre Company). He has worked extensively at The Ark, where he recently directed *No Messin' with the Monkeys* by Roddy Doyle. Louis has composed music and was musical director for *The Lost Days of Ollie Deasy* (Macnas) and also on *Bumbógs and Bees* (TEAM). TV includes: *Killinascully, Showbands* and *The Morbegs* (RTE 1). On radio he played Nick in *Who's afraid of Viginia Woolf* (RTE Radio 1).

Fergal McElherron
FRANK HAYES

Theatre includes: *Rudolf the Red* (The Ark), *Savoy* (Peacock Theatre), *Olga* (Rough Magic), *Mixing it on the Mountain* (Calypso), *Candide* (Performance Corporation) – Best Actor, Dublin Fringe Festival and Best Supporting Actor, Irish Times/ESB Theatre Awards 2002, *Trainspotting* (Common Currency), *Iphigenia At Aulis* (Abbey), *Why I Hate The Circus* (Green Light Productions), *Starchild and Other Stories* (Storytellers), *The House* (Abbey), *Mojo Mickybo* (Kabosh) – Best Actor, Dublin Fringe Festival and Best Actor nomination, Irish Times/ESB Theatre Awards 1998, *Shoot the Crow* (Druid). Film and TV: *The Anarchic Hand Affair* (RTE Short Cuts), *The Clinic* (RTE), *Omagh* (UTV), *Holy Cross* (BBC/RTE), *H3* (Stanbury Films), *Eureka Street* (Euphoria Films), *The Secret of Roan Inish* (Skerry Movies).

Janet Moran
MAGGIE

Theatre work includes *The Hostage*, *The Well of the Saints*, *Barbaric Comedies*, *Communion*, *She Stoops to Conquer* and *The Cherry Orchard* all at The Abbey and The Peacock. Janet has also played in *Stella by Starlight* (The Gate), *Car Show* (The Corn Exchange), *The Stomping Ground* (Red Kettle), *Royal Supreme* (Theatre Royal Plymouth), *Dancing at Lughnasa* (An Grianán), *Dead Funny* (Rough Magic), *Love and Understanding* (Purple Heart) and *Xaviers* (Calipo Theatre Company, of which she is an associate artist). TV and film: *Career Opportunities* (RTE/BBC), *Moll Flanders*, *Nothing Personal*, *The Butcher Boy* and the series *Love is the Drug* (RTE).

Mark O'Halloran
MARTYN WALLACE

Mark O'Halloran is from Ennis, Co. Clare, and is a graduate of The Gaiety School of Acting. Theatre work includes *As You Like It*, *Salome*, *Terese Raquin*, *Christmas Carol*, *Pride and Prejudice*, *Arms and The Man* and *Lady Windermere's Fan* (all at The Gate). He has also worked with Druid, Guna Nua, Peacock and with The Corn Exchange in The Seagull and Car Show. Television and film credits include *Paths to Freedom*, *H3* and *Adam and Paul* (which he also wrote).

Margarita Corscadden
STAGE DIRECTOR

Recent productions include *Monged* (Fishamble Theatre Co), *As You Like It* (Classic Stage Ireland), *Many Happy Returns* (The Gate), *Like Silver* (Irish Modern Dance Theatre), *Savoy* at The Peacock, *Earthfalls and Revolutions* at Project, *Moll* (Edward Farrell Productions), which went to New York and Boston followed by a nationwide tour. She is delighted to be working with The Corn Exchange.

Des Kenny
PRODUCTION MANAGER

Recent credits include *Tadhg Stray Wandered In* and *Monged* (Fishamble), *Far Away* (Bedrock), *Alone it Stands* (Lane Productions and Yew Tree Theatre Company), *Triple Espresso* (Lane Productions) and *Mud* (The Corn Exchange), which won the Irish Times ESB Irish Theatre Award for Best Production 2003.

Lisa Mahony
STAGE MANAGER

Lisa graduated last year from the BA in Drama and Theatre Studies at Trinity College, Dublin. Recent stage management credits include *Come Good Rain* at the Samuel Beckett Theatre, Dublin and The Spiegeltent during the 2004 Dublin Fringe Festival. Having spent last year's Fringe working at The Traverse she is delighted to be back again this year.

Rob Furey
RELIGHTING DESIGN

Rob Furey has worked in all aspects of theatre industry for the past twelve years – touring worldwide with theatre companies and in the rock 'n' roll industry. Rob trained in the The Abbey Theatre in Ireland learning lighting. He has a degree in sound engineering and has been a freelance production manager for the past four years. He loves having the craic!

Sarah Durcan
PRODUCER

Sarah holds a BA in Communications from DCU. She has worked with The Corn Exchange since graduating with a MA in Cultural Policy and Arts Management from UCD. She co-produced *Mud*, and produced *Dublin by Lamplight* (premiere 2004, Irish tour 2005, and for the Edinburgh Fringe 2005).

Popcorn

Great to taste, even better to share...

By joining Popcorn, our friends' initiative, not only will you be supporting The Corn Exchange's radically different form of theatre, you will also have priority access to a range of events and happenings each year.

Annual Popcorn membership offers more benefits than ever before, including complimentary tickets, priority booking, quarterly email newsletter, member's pre-show talk, acknowledgement in all programmes and escorted small parties to theatre and other arts events. Membership offers value for money and is also a great gift idea.

Regular (Individual) €100 per annum
Student (Concession) €40 per annum
Large (Patron) €500+ per annum
Supersize €1,000+ per annum

Your membership allows The Corn Exchange to develop our style of theatre further and invest in our writers, directors and actors. To find out more about becoming a Popcorn member, or to join our mailing list and receive regular updates on our productions, please contact:

The Corn Exchange,
43-44 Temple Bar,
Dublin 2, Ireland.
T +353 1 679 6444

Email info@cornexchange.ie
or log on to www.cornexchange.ie

The Corn Exchange is a charity registered in Ireland CHY 15490.

Dublin by Lamplight

Introduction

Dublin, 1904, is associated with two cultural touchstones: the founding of the Abbey Theatre and the setting for Joyce's *Ulysses*.

There is a pleasing symmetry to the pairing of the two: the night of 27 December when the Abbey first opened its doors to the public is an attested fact, built on a myth of Ireland's past. 16 June is now remembered for what never happened, but its invention is scrupulously based on the actuality of what Ireland had become.

In any case, our initial inspiration in making *Dublin by Lamplight* was to collapse these shibboleths together and tell the story of an amateur drama group trying to establish a National Theatre, and tell it as the story of a single day.

Perhaps coincidentally Annie Ryan, the artistic director of The Corn Exchange, was keen to explore a similar collision stylistically: between the brutal enactment that is *commedia dell'arte* and the lyrical narrative that makes Story Theatre.

This partly grew out of an anomaly which had been noted in workshops: that characters could do anything or go anywhere in improvisation, but the search for performable material led almost invariably to the well-made, one-location play. We were keen to take the form outdoors, as it were, and hear what the characters might be thinking to themselves.

Early twentieth-century Dublin seemed uniquely suited to this challenge. From the poverty to the politics, the literature to the excrement, the period is fetid with myth-making and obsessed with the birth of a nation. Theatrically it was like imagining a silent movie with dialogue.

*

In 1892 a Parliamentary Select Committee on Theatres and Places of Entertainment produced the following exchange:

Q. *As a matter of fact, I suppose the Irish are not great theatregoers?*

A. *They are.*

Q. *But there are only two theatres in Dublin.*

A. *Yes.*

These two were the Gaiety and the Queen's, and there were only six more theatres on the rest of the island. (London, by comparison, had around forty theatres and the same number of large music halls.)

By 1904 the number had swelled to three with the reopening of the Theatre Royal, but indigenous theatre companies would never have been able to fill these auditoria. A variety of meeting halls and unsuitable spaces were pressed into occasional service – the Antient Concert Rooms, Molesworth Hall, even St Teresa's Temperance Hall on Clarendon Street – but if these are recalled now it is for the curiosity of having hosted the premieres of many more celebrated plays.

Which leads back to the theme of *Dublin by Lamplight.* Whatever about having a National Theatre without a building, can you have one without a nation? Indeed, can there only be one National Theatre? Would it not be more patriotic to establish your own?

In the Dublin of the time, this was not an idle question. The city was crawling with rival drama groups – juggling the same words in their title, and frequently the same personnel in their company – all striving to be the first to establish their National Theatre.

The main obstacle was simple. The establishment of a new dedicated theatre required a patent from the Lord Lieutenant of Ireland, and this the existing theatres strenuously opposed. The reason Yeats and the Abbey succeeded was Lady Gregory. She had the required influence and a patent was granted to perform 'plays in the Irish or English language, written by Irish writers on Irish subjects and selected by the Irish National Theatre Society.' For the record, she also agreed not to put on stage any exhibition of wild beasts, 'or to allow women or children to be hung from the flies or fixed in positions from which they cannot release themselves'.

This was the cultural recreation of a people who had neither independence nor home rule.

And whatever about the clout of Lady Gregory or indeed Cathleen Ni Houlihan, neither did they have universal suffrage, something they shared with their cousins across the Irish Sea.

And yet, in spite of Yeats' famous question ('Did that play of mine send out / Certain men the English shot?') it would be a mistake to overstate the importance of theatre in all this. For even if the Abbey became a notorious or illustrious flashpoint during the *Playboy* riots of 1907, from the point of view of the newspapers and the pulpits the main recreational hazard was alcohol. Although a casual scrutiny of the figures gathered by Joseph O'Brien indicates that while alcoholism might have been a problem, affording it was simply out of the reach of the vast majority of the citizens.

It is hard to comprehend the poverty of what was once the empire's second city. Dublin's population in 1904 comprised some 300,000 people. A third of the city's families lived in one-room tenements – but even this does not convey the dreadful reality.

The legal definition of overcrowding was less than 400 cubic feet per adult, half that per child. This means that a not untypical room, 16ft x 16ft x 10ft, was not overcrowded if it was inhabited by no more than five adults and three children.

Under laws regulating the many dairies and cowsheds in the city, a cow in her byre was entitled to 800 cubic feet.

There is a much-repeated statistic that Dublin's death rate at this time was comparable to that of Calcutta. In 1899 this meant 33.6 deaths per thousand living, exceeding that of any city in Europe or the United States, and representing an annual waste of some 3,500 lives compared with mortality rates in London or Edinburgh.

This situation had improved somewhat by 1904, but preventable diseases still accounted for over one third of all deaths in Dublin.

One in three deaths was of a child under five.

And the city stank. It produced twice the filth of larger cities such as Edinburgh or even London. The River Liffey was effectively a giant cesspool for the collection of sewage: excreta of humans and animals, road-sweepings and industrial waste all drained directly into it and oozed slowly into Dublin Bay. At high tide the main sewers were closed by the tidal valves causing blockages and leaks back up the system; at low tide the smell got worse, to the extent that men with brooms were sent to scrub the exposed sides of the river of whatever deposits could be dropped back into the water.[1]

That we now remember this Dublin for the output of its writers is a tribute to the quality as well as the quantity of their emissions.

*

Our play is called a collaboration because of the circumstances surrounding its creation. Specifically, this means that we assembled a cast, a creative team and a devising period before committing anything to paper other than the premise alluded to at the beginning of this account.

We knew there would be a play-within-a-play and that it would be set on the day the King came to town. After four weeks of whatever it is you do in development, we had the principal characters and large swathes of the action, and we tried staging what we discovered as both 'pure' *commedia* (with mask and fixed location) and 'pure' Story Theatre (whatever you could find or invent). Towards the end, with

1 These figures are taken from a marvellous book, *Dear, Dirty Dublin: a City in Distress, 1899-1916* by Joseph V. O'Brien.

the addition of the live music provided by Conor Linehan, we were lucky to experience one of those perfect ensemble days where everything came together. This was immensely depressing precisely because of the realisation that we would spend the rest of our time together trying to recapture that feeling.

A Technical Note

Dublin by Lamplight includes over thirty characters played by six actors; the distribution of parts is indicated by the groupings of characters on page 8. The [Castle Agent] and the [British Soldier] are voices heard from off; the [Huzzar] is performed by the actor playing Willy without a costume change or leaving the stage. The text consists of attributed dialogue, but also employs third-person narration. The narration is to be delivered by the actor in character at full emotional tilt.

All props – except for Frank's leather bag and its contents – are imaginary, or mimed, whichever is the less offensive term.

It is also worth pointing out that the six actors wear fixed painted masks, but undergo complete costume changes for each character. I still don't know how they do this, but witnessing it has been one of the many pleasures I have enjoyed along the way.

Michael West
Dublin, June 2005

Characters

Martyn Wallace
Dung Dodger 2
Maloney
Waster 1
Constable Flower
Doherty
Whore 1
Mendicant

Maggie
Mrs Madden
Nora
Small Boy
Whore 3

Eva St John
Passerby
Floozie in Bar
Whore 2

Willy Hayes
Angry Mother
Sergeant Kearns
Barman
[Huzzar]

Frank Hayes
Maggie's Mother
Dung Dodger 1
Inspector Trench
[Castle Agent]
[British Soldier]

Jimmy Finnegan
Boylan
Waster 2
Mr Nobbs
Constable Eddie

Act One

The City

Scene One

Boarding house.

Martyn   Martyn Wallace awoke in his boarding house and held his aching head. His room was brown and dirty and bare. He called it Reading Gaol.

In nomine Patris, et Filii, et Spiritus Sancti . . . Oh, and one more thing. Please remember to shower down your blessings on my opening. Thank you.

Now he had to make good his escape, without encountering that handbag Mrs Madden.

He creeps out, only to run into the offending article.

Mrs Madden   Mr Wallace.

Martyn   Mrs Madden, I apologise for my behaviour last night. And I must ask your indulgence for the week's rent in arrears.

Mrs Madden   Will you be late home tonight?

Martyn   It's our premiere. We may celebrate with a cup of soup.

Mrs Madden   If you come home drunk again, you can consider yourself in requirement of other accommodation.

Exit **Martyn Wallace**.

Scene Two

Georgian morning room.

Nora, *a servant girl, wheels in a trolley to her mistress.*

Eva   Eva St John, actress, benefactress, activist, took her breakfast in the morning room, a little earlier than usual. Four slices of dry toast . . .

Nora   No crusts.

Eva   . . . and an apple.

With a pearl-handled fruit knife she peeled it in a single jagged spiral and tossed the skin over her shoulder to see what letter it would make on the carpet. This was something young girls did to find the name of their beloved and Eva was feeling slightly giddy today. (*She inspects the peel.*)

An S? What could it mean? S for . . . sister. Sign.

Nora   Surprise?

Eva   Quite possibly, Nora. I have it! An S for Yes. Could you bring in that item I ordered from Weirs. Just place it on the mantel in the drawing room.

Exit **Nora** *with a curtsy.*

Eva   And could you fetch me a hammer? Thank you.

Eva purred to herself. It was going to be a wonderful day!

Exit **Eva**.

Scene Three

Tenement. Wailing infants. **Maggie** *and her* **Ma**, *who slops some porridge into a bowl.*

Maggie   Maggie looked at the porridge. It was watery and grey.

I can't do it, Ma.

Ma   Eat.

Maggie   I can't.

Ma   I've nothing else for you.

Maggie   Me stomach is at me, is all. I'll eat something at work. They'll give me something in the kitchen.

Ma   Will you be able to help me tonight?

Maggie   I can't, I'm . . . meeting someone.

Ma   I hope you're not going to the theatre. You shouldn't be wasting your time with people the like of them.

Maggie   No, Mother.

Ma   And we're behind in the rent. Haven't they paid you?

Maggie   I'll get it tonight.

Ma   And if you're not feeling well you should come home and help me with the extra laundry. With the King and all coming, everybody wants to be washing themselves, it seems.

Maggie   I can't, Mother. I'll do it tomorrow.

Ma   The King'll be gone tomorrow, won't he? He'll be in some far off place the like of Killarney or Malahide.

Maggie   But Maggie wasn't listening. She was only thinking of tonight and Frank. Frank!

Ma   I don't know, girl. If I didn't know you better I'd say you were . . . Oh Maggie. You're not, are you?

Maggie   I'm late for work.

Ma   Maggie! Maggie, come back here and tell me you're not having a . . .

Exit **Maggie**.

The **Ma** *shrieks.*

Scene Four

The Hayes brothers' house.

Frank   Frank woke with a shout. He had fallen asleep in his clothes, he'd bitten the inside of his cheek in his sleep and his throat was sore. He'd dreamt it again. That he wouldn't be able to do it. That his nerve would fail him at the last hurdle.

Willy?

Enter **Willy Hayes**.

Willy   Willy was his brother. Elder brother.

What's wrong with you, Frank? Nightmares, is it?

Frank   Frank drank a little whiskey, to calm himself down.

What time is it?

Willy   Let me see, said Willy. Seven minutes past eight. We should be up. I'm up.

And how up! Today was the day of reckoning, the day of destiny, the day the Irish National Theatre of Ireland would take her place among . . .

Frank *stumbles groggily past him, tripping over the newspaper.*

Willy   The paper.

He turns through the paper more and more anxiously.

Frank *makes the toilet where he violently pukes.*

Willy   Are you sure you placed that ad like I told you?

Frank   What ad?

Willy   The ad. Did you remember to place that ad?

Frank   Oh, the ad. Course I did.

Willy   Well, where is it?

With a cry of relief he locates a small announcement.

'Tonight, in its debut presentation, the Irish National Theatre of Ireland presents: a play by William Hayes. *The Wooing of Emer.* Doors open . . . ' The Wowing of Emer. Frank! It says 'The Wowing of Emer.'

Frank   It's a misprint.

Willy   You're a misprint.

Frank   Will you make me a cup of tea?

Willy   There isn't any tea.

Frank   Is there any milk?

Willy   No. Is there any change from the money I gave you?

Frank   I spent it.

Willy   Never mind.

Willy tried to saw some stale bread he had discovered under a tea towel on the sideboard. Oh my God, the time! It was almost nine. He was going to be late. You were never late for Miss St John. For Eva. She was a demon for punctuality. And for a meeting of this importance . . . Where's the lease? The lease!

Willy *finds the lease.*

He pressed it to his chest as the room began to turn once more. To give his company a permanent home. To announce, before all the others, the arrival of the Irish National Theatre of Ireland. To go down in history as the −

Frank *taps him on the shoulder.*

Frank   Can I borrow your bag?

Willy   My Gladstone? You're not going anywhere, are you?

Frank   I need it.

Willy   Remember, Frank. This is the moment of truth. Tonight you go before our countrymen to strike a blow for freedom, for nationhood. Tonight you're going to act for Ireland.

Frank *(hoarsely)*   For Ireland.

Willy   And watch that throat, said Willy as he swept out the door.

Exit **Frank**.

Scene Five

Willy *strolls through the streets.*

Willy   Dublin was a fine city this day of Our Lord MCMIV.
Famous for its wit. Its intimate charm. Perhaps a little light
in its appreciation of the performing arts.

He sings:

  I'm trotting o'er the cobblestones of Dublin,
  Bedecked with memories of yesteryear.
  A tram runs by with a ting-ting-ting,
  A little boy begins to sing,
  I'm trotting o'er the cobblestones of –

He steps in dog shit.

Dublin.

He exits, passing two **Dung Dodgers** *in overalls.*

Dodger 1   With a suck and a splat . . .

Dodger 2   Two Dung Dodgers shovelled the manure and
ash from the stinking mountain before the tenements into a
dirty dray.

Dodger 1   Good consistency.

Dodger 2   You could almost tell what they had for dinner.

Dodger 1   If they had any dinner. Most of it's like . . .
soup.

Dodger 2   If it's not the little pebbles it's the soup.

Dodger 1   You'd think if they had the dysentery you'd
make twice as much.

Dodger 2   I never liked the dysentery for the slop of it.

Boy   A little boy ran out.

Are yous dung dodgers?

His **Angry Mother** *emerges and clips him over the ear.*

Angry Mother   Come away from them, or we'll be late for the King. (*To* **Dodgers**.) It's only because His Majesty is in town that you're cleaning that muck at all. We nearly drowned in it last week. There's that nice Jimmy Finnegan.

Boy   All right, Jimmy?

Passerby   Morning, Jimmy.

Jimmy *saunters past the others as they leave.*

Jimmy   Morning!

By College Green, the wind took Jimmy's cap. It landed at the foot of a street lamp. On the lamp was hanging a little basket, a bouquet of roses. Someone must have put them out for the King – he was going to pass right by this spot in a few hours. The dew was still glistening on the petals.

An abandoned ladder was leaning against the lamp post; the fellow must have been caught short. Jimmy looked around him and stepped quickly up the rungs and plucked a rose. Soft as skin, as Maggie's rosy face, her blush the time he tried to kiss her. She'd turned away.

He sings a heartfelt lovesong.

Have you felt the pain, my boys, O have you felt the pain.
I'd rather be in gaol, I would, than be in love again.
The girl I love is beautiful, I'll have you all to know,
For I met her in the garden where the praties grow.

This was her rose. He hid it carefully inside his jacket and hurried off to the theatre.

Exit **Jimmy**.

Scene Six

Eva's Georgian rooms.

Eva   Eva was waiting for Willy in a rose-coloured room, standing before the large sash window.

Enter **Willy**.

Eva   You're late.

Willy   Many apologies, Eva. The crowds . . .

Eva   The omens are with us, William. I received a message.

Willy   A message?

Eva   From the other side.

Willy   What did it say?

Eva   S.

Willy   S?

Eva   For Yes. And that is why I am prepared to sign the lease for the Irish National Theatre of Ireland. Our life's work needs a home.

Willy   Willy's empty stomach skipped skywards with a surge of joy. He saw white lights dance before his eyes.

Eva   Now give me your watch.

Willy   I beg your pardon?

Eva   Your watch. Give it me.

Willy   Gingerly, Willy handed over his father's watch. And watched with surprise . . .

Eva   As Eva carefully placed it in a handkerchief and smashed it with a hammer.

Now look behind you, on the mantel.

Willy   Willy dizzily turned to find a little blue hinged case embossed in gold. It opened with a tiny creak to reveal a beautiful gold fob-watch and chain.

Eva   The old order is over. This watch is to mark the start of a new era, a new Eire, a new time, for theatre, for nationhood, for freedom. And to remind you never to be late again.

Willy   I don't know what to say.

Eva   There's an inscription.

Willy   William pressed the catch and tried to read the writing.

Eva   'To Darling William. All my love, Eva.'

Willy   It swam before him and he felt faint.

Eva   I know, I feel the same way, William.

They sing an aria of hunger and longing, singing simultaneously (indicated by /).

Eva   Oh William, oh William, I hunger for your love /

Willy   William, he wanted just two slices of bread.

Eva   Though you think me foolish, it's in the stars above /

Willy   Then he could place them on either side of her tasty little head.

Eva   I want you to feed me and then − /

Willy   And eat her with relish, mayonnaise and −

Willy *raises her hand to his lips and prepares to devour it.* **Eva** *breaks away*

Eva   We mustn't, William. Not here. First we must solemnise our contract, we must sign the lease.

Willy   The lease, the lease.

She takes the lease from him and puts it away in a bureau.

Eva   I will sign the lease later, with my solicitor. Now all that remains is to pay the dreadful McKenzie his rent and the deed will be done. How much is it for again?

Willy   I believe it's ten pounds.

Eva   Ten pounds? A pittance.

Willy   A pittance? Perhaps this would be an auspicious time to ask for a small loan.

Eva   Ten pounds for the freedom of our souls.

Willy   Eva. I don't quite know how to put this, but would you be offended if . . .

She stops writing her cheque.

Eva   William. What am I doing? How thoughtless of me.

Willy   Not at all, Eva, it's just . . .

Eva   Your soul can't be bought like a cheap bolt of cloth.

Willy   No, but I . . .

Eva   No, you're right. We are partners, colleagues and equals. We have shared everything and we must share this too.

Willy   Thank you, Eva.

Eva   I will sign the lease. You must pay the ten pounds. (*She tears up the cheque.*)

Willy   I pay the ten pounds? But I haven't a . . .

Eva   Not another word. William Hayes is not for sale. Now I'm off to rally the sisters for our demonstration against the King. The Daughters of Erin await me. And of course I must prepare my final speech as Emer. Such a wonderful speech. Until tonight, Willy!

Exit **Eva**.

Scene Seven

Sackville Street.

Willy   Willy alighted from the tram at Nelson's Pillar, where all the lines converged. He flicked away his blue tram ticket and counted out the four lonely pennies that comprised his worldly fortune. Fourpence! How he was going to find ten pounds? Ten pounds! Perhaps he would have to marry her.

He had to eat something immediately or he was going to pass out.

Exit.

Scene Eight

Nassau Hotel bedroom.

Maggie   Maggie was on her eighth room in the Nassau Hotel. Dusting and tidying and emptying bins and washing the floor and stripping the beds and making the beds.

And the wind and sun among the leaves in the trees in College Park outside the window caught her eye. She saw crowds lining the streets, hoping for a glimpse of the King. She could imagine their happy smiling faces looking up at her, admiring her.

She imagines herself onstage in her finest hour.

'People of Ireland, rise.'

She thought of Frank, she imagined what it would be like sharing the stage with him. What it would be like lying in bed beside him.

Not like the last time.

Oh Frank . . .

Exit.

Scene Nine

Hayes' house bathroom. **Frank** *is staring grimly in the mirror.*

Frank   . . . took Willy's razor and began to shave. The water was cold.

He nicked his cheek: the sharp sting and the warm blood trickling down the side of his face and into the washbasin, drip, drip, each drop hitting the water in a slow explosion of red.

Exit.

Scene Ten

Stephen's Green.

Martyn   In Stephen's Green, Martyn stood on the arched bridge over the lake like Priam upon the battlements. Scenting the wind of change, he surveyed the gathering forces. What drama was going to be unleashed upon the world?

A gentleman in a long coat approaches.

Trench   It looks like the sky is clearing.

Martyn   A little tent of blue.

Trench   Would this be a good vantage point to view the passing of the King?

Martyn   Is he sick? Forgive me, I have a dark humour.

Trench   I would like to follow the route His Majesty will be taking.

Martyn   Be born into a wealthy family and die of gout. Or you could look out for the little blue and red flags.

Trench   You are not a Unionist.

Martyn   Sir, I am an artist. Tell me, are you interested in the theatre at all? Say you are, because tonight . . .

He escorts him off.

Scene Eleven

Hayes' house. **Frank** *produces a leather bag.*

Frank   From under the bed, Frank took out Willy's brown leather bag.

He reveals a hiding place in the floor.

Next, he lifted the loose floorboard and carefully transferred five neatly wrapped sticks of gelignite and laid them side by side in Willy's bag, like sausages in paper.

He covered them with a wrinkled shirt and a copy of the *United Irishman*. He cleared his throat.

For Ireland.

Exit.

Scene Twelve

Bewley's Café.

Willy   Willy Hayes sat in Bewley's, Westmoreland Street, like a sultan of the Orient. Before him on a plain white plate sat the burnt offering his last earthly pence afforded him. A sausage.

The indignity. A man of his talent and calling. And not a shilling to his name. He tried to shut out all thoughts of ten pounds. Ten pounds! How was he going to find ten pounds? What time was it? He looked at his new gold watch . . .

What was he thinking? It was a gift. He couldn't possibly.

Could he?

No, it was out of the question.

Was it?

He couldn't.

Yes, he could.

Forgive me Eva, I do it for Ireland.

He threw back his tea in a scalding rush and popped the sausage into his jacket pocket. He had to get to the pawnshop.

He runs outside.

What were all these people doing? Of course, the bloody King! He pushed past the loyal subjects. Excuse me. Excuse me! And ran smack dab into a wall of horseflesh, the flank of an enormous beast, on top of which sat . . .

Huzzar   A huzzar of the Royal Dublin Fusiliers, in frock coat and helmet, an outrider for the King's carriage.

How's it going, darling?

Willy   Get off your bloody horse and fight for your own country, why don't you? *Eire abu*. You lickspittle.

And he gave the horse's rump a slap.

The horse took a start and its hooves clopped violently on the cobbles. But, tucking his cane under his arm, Willy was off.

Exit.

Scene Thirteen

Grafton Street.

Eva   Eva met Martyn as arranged at the top of Grafton Street.

Dia dhuit, a chara.

Martyn   Darling.

Eva   We've been to the Mansion House to deliver our petition to the King. The girls will be strategically placed along the route.

Martyn   Eva, you are indefatigable.

Eva   Now all we have to do is chain ourselves to the railings outside Trinity.

Martyn   How exciting.

Eva   Eva fixed her hat and prepared to meet her fate.

Martyn, we're ready.

Martyn   I'm right behind you.

Eva   They plunged into the crowds.

No recruitment, no conscription. Up the Boers! Down with the King!

Martyn   Martyn marched beside her and marvelled at her. All around them were the daughters of Erin, the *Inghinidhe na hEireann,* and a whole tide of indifference, hostility and men.

Eva   But Eva pushed through them all.

Sons of Erin, listen to your sisters. Do not fight for the imperial powers. Join the struggle for Ireland.

Martyn   Martyn tried to keep up.

Eva   Martyn, can you see their faces? Their hope, their hunger?

Eva reached the front of Trinity College. The crowds were surging around her, jostling her, jeering her. Someone tried to knock off her hat, but she stood firm.

Martyn   A small cavalcade of soldiers on horseback clopped by, the pale sun glinting on their brocades. The little blue and red flags flickered with excitement as they passed.

It's the King!

Eva   Now, Martyn, chain me to the railings.

Martyn   There seem to be a lot of policemen.

Voice   Up the Boers! Down with the King!

Voice   God Save the King! Your Majesty, over here!

Martyn   The police were brandishing their batons.

They charged!

They broke into the crowd.

People tried to scatter.

But it was impossible.

The others sweep across, taking **Eva** *with them.*

Martyn *is suddenly alone.*

Martyn   Scuffling, shouting, pushing, pushing.

And when Martyn turned around –

Eva was gone!

Exit.

Scene Fourteen

The King's statue, Dame Street.

Frank   Caught up in the stampeding mob, Frank held tight to his bag.

He ducked behind the pedestal of the large bronze statue and took shelter. People streamed past on either side. The cold dark metal lowered above him. His foreshortened Majesty condescending to him, belittling him. Frank could feel the rage grip him by the throat.

I'll show you. Your time has come.

– Ja want to buy me flag? came a voice from behind the bronze knees.

A small boy had climbed the pedestal to see down the street. He held a Union Jack. He had no shoes.

Frank clasped his bag to his chest and ran away from the statue, the boy, the street . . .

Exit.

Scene Fifteen

Willy *flees down an alley.*

Willy   . . . the crowds. He had to get away. Looking over his shoulder to make sure he wasn't being followed, Willy took a precautionary jag down a lane.

He stops.

It was prehistorically dark and a large greasy puddle lay the length of it. Willy wasn't sure if this was a lane that gave out onto the street with the pawnbroker, or was it only a dead end?

He turns to leave but two **IRB Men** *block his path.*

Boylan   Good day to you, sir.

Willy   Good day, men.

Maloney   Do you mind?

He relieves **Willy** *of his cane.*

Willy   My cane.

Boylan   May I?

Willy   That's my watch.

Boylan   'To darling William, all my love, Eva.' Very nice of her.

Willy   Yes. That's rather special to me. You're tearing the button hole.

Boylan   Apologies.

He pockets his watch while **Maloney** *pats him down.*

Willy   I have nothing in my pockets, I assure you.

Maloney   What's this?

Willy   That's a sausage.

Boylan *removes his wallet.*

Willy   But that wallet, I promise you, is unfortunately empty. Not my cane!

Maloney *deftly snaps it in two on his knee.*

Maloney   Tell Frank we're looking for him.

Boylan   Ponce.

They shove him to the ground.

Willy   Who are you?

The **IRB Men** *slink away as* **Willy** *lands in the puddle.*

Willy   My poor theatre. Help! Police!

Exit **Willy**.

Scene Sixteen

College Green.

Martyn   Eva! Eva!

He'd let her down, he'd pledged to watch over her and she had been plucked from under his very nose.

And then he saw the pointed helmets of two constables disappearing through the hordes. He was sure he caught a glimpse of Eva's feathered hat between them.

Eva, Eva, I'm coming.

His Helen had been taken from him, he would avenge her.

And then it dawned on him: they had taken her to Troy. She was being detained in Brunswick Street Police Station.

He pushes the door into . . .

Scene Seventeen

The Police Station. **Constable Kearns** *is talking to an unseen colleague.*

Kearns   Are you disappointed you got desk duty today, Harry? I said are you disappointed . . . You're disappointed. Well, man. It's not the worst. I remember one time we were in Baltinglass and this fellow . . .

Martyn *taps the desk.*

Martyn   Where is Miss St John, whom I saw manhandled?

Kearns   What is it, man?

Martyn   You must release Miss St John, whom you have wrongly imprisoned.

Kearns   Harry, we've a right one here. Who's this you say we're holding?

Martyn   Miss Eva St John. You must let her go.

Kearns   Well now. If she did nothing wrong, she wouldn't be here. How do you spell . . . What's this her name is?

Martyn   Miss St John.

Kearns   What class of a name is that, at all?

The large Dublin Metropolitan Policeman reached for the duty book.

He opened the massive tome.

A cloud of dust rises, which he flaps away. Exit **Martyn***.*

Scene Eighteen

Palace Bar.

Barman   A beam of dusty sunlight transfixed the counter where a fat barman polished glasses and blinked.

Customers materialise out of the darkness, including **Frank** *and his bag.*

Frank   Frank was having a drink in the Palace Bar to steady himself. He tried to ignore the floozy and a pair of wasters who decorated the mahogany, a bas-relief of dissolute life and everything his brother abhorred. He counted out the last of Willy's money and ordered another whiskey.

Waster 1   One of the men sidled over to him.

Stand us one, will ya? For the day that's in it and all.

Frank   Frank gave him a coin and tried to return to his drink.

Waster 1   God bless you. To the King.

A deathly silence descends.

Waster 2   To Ireland! shouted his companion from up the bar.

Waster 1   Yes, to Ireland. Sweet Erin go brea.

Waster 2   Which is it, Furey? You old bellows.

Waster 1   Don't mind you.

Waster 2   Which is it, Furey? Cathleen Ni Houlihan? Or that old German bugger with the moustache?

Waster 1   You watch yourself, Daly. I'm having a drink with me old comrade here.

Waster 2   Coming over here to raise an army against the poor Boers. Sure what did they ever do to anyone?

Waster 1   That's it. I'll show you.

The **Wasters** *fight and drag each other off.*

Woman   Do you be needing company? said the woman, slinking over.

Frank   Frank bristled in alarm. She seemed part liquid, part tentacle.

Frank *extracts himself from her attentions.*

Maloney *and* **Boylan***, the two* **IRB Men***, arrive and clear the bar.*

Maloney   Hello, Frank. Been looking for you.

Frank   Looking for me?

Boylan   Fancy finding you here.

Frank   Just having a quiet drink.

Maloney   Just having a drink, is it?

Frank   Yeah.

Maloney   For the day that's in it.

Frank   That'd be it, yeah.

Maloney   Looks like it's going to be nice.

Frank   Clearing up, yeah.

Maloney   A bit of rain earlier, but looking nice now.

Frank   And a bit of wind.

Maloney   Oh yes, a bit of wind. Keeps the flags flying.

Frank   For the King?

Maloney *grabs him by the lapels.*

Maloney   Listen, Frank, you watch yourself, all right?

Boylan   We've heard things about you, Frank.

Frank   I only meant . . .

Maloney   Never mind what you meant. We want you to keep your nose clean, Frank.

Boylan   This is not the time, do you understand?

Maloney   The organisation won't tolerate any sort of rogue acting.

Boylan   What are you up to, Frank?

Frank   I'm doing a play.

Boylan   A play, is it?

Frank   Written by the brother. You should see it.

Maloney   What's it called?

Frank   *The Wooing of Emer.*

Maloney   Gaelic, is it?

Frank   No. *The Wooing* . . . the wooing.

Boylan   The whatting?

Maloney   There's nothing . . . improper about it, is there?

Frank   God, no. It's about Ireland. You'd like it.

Maloney   Are there peasants?

Frank   No, mythical heroes.

Maloney   And who are you?

Frank   I'm Cuchulain.

Maloney   You're Cuchulain.

The **IRB Men** *exit, laughing.*

Frank   Yes. We're doing it tonight. I'll get you tickets, no problem.

Exit **Frank**.

Scene Nineteen

Sackville Street.

Willy   What has this country come to if we must cower in the alleys of our national citadel? Is this the protection promised us by England? What serves us now, all the police and soldiery trooping through our native land if you can't find a bloody policeman when you need one?

Constable Flower *appears.*

Flower   Not making a political statement, are we?

Willy   No, no. I've been assaulted. They stole my watch.

Flower   Describe it.

Willy   Gold, fob, roman numerals, twenty-four carat, eighteen jewels, engraved in fetching cursive 'To darling William, all my love, Eva.'

Flower   A gold watch. I see.

Willy   And they broke my cane.

Flower   Describe it.

Willy   Black, silver handle, Duchard et fils, Montmartre, engraved '*Pour mon semblable, mon frère.*' Broken.

Flower   A black cane. I see.

Willy   And my wallet. Pigskin. Brown.

Flower   Brown, I see. And how much was in it?

Willy (*pause*)   Ten pounds.

Flower   That's a very serious crime.

Willy   Yes it is.

Flower   I'm going to have to take your particulars. Your name?

Scene Twenty

Nassau Hotel.

Maggie   Maggie, sir.

Nobbs   Well, Maggie. There's no question of being paid until the end of the month. And you're on the late shift tonight.

Maggie   Not tonight, sir, Mr Nobbs, I can't.

Nobbs   You can't? Don't you need the extra money?

Maggie   Please, not tonight, sir. I was promised to be let off early.

Nobbs   Wanting to see the King, like all the others.

Maggie   No, sir, Mr Nobbs. I have to be at the theatre.

Nobbs   The theatre? I'm afraid no girl working under me can be permitted any association with the theatre.

Maggie   I'm just doing the costumes.

Nobbs   I will have to terminate your position with us.

Maggie   Don't do that, sir, please. I'll do anything, anything, but please let me go.

Nobbs   What's your name again?

Maggie *and* **Nobbs** *exit.*

Scene Twenty-One

Police station.

Martyn   Martyn Wallace.

Kearns   Do I know you?

Martyn   Possibly. I'm an actor.

Kearns   Go away. Where, in the Empire?

Martyn   Once. I did *The Corsican Brothers*.

Kearns   Did you? Wait, you were . . . You were in it!

Martyn   Well, yes, I was.

Kearns   What's your name again?

Martyn   Martyn Wallace.

Kearns   Harry, Eddie, get out here, you'll never guess who's after coming in.

Enter **Constable Eddie**.

Eddie   Who is it?

Kearns   It's Martyn Wallace.

Eddie   What's he done?

Martyn   Various things.

Eddie   Is he turning himself in?

Kearns   No, Martyn Wallace, the actor.

Eddie   Oh!

Kearns   *The Corsican Brothers*.

Eddie   May I shake your hand?

Martyn   You saw it?

Eddie   The whole station saw it. Didn't we? Harry, get out here, you're missing it!

Kearns   What can we do for you, Mr Wallace?

Martyn   I'm here to escort Miss Eva St John from your custody.

Eddie   She's in here, is she?

Martyn   Yes, she's here by mistake.

Kearns   We don't make mistakes.

Martyn   Of course not. There's a misunderstanding, that's all.

Eddie   She broke the law.

Martyn   It was a trifle, a piddling offence.

Kearns   No, it says here: pamphleteering.

Eddie   And chaining herself to property.

Kearns   That's a tricky one.

Eddie   The day that's in it and all.

Martyn   Yes, but we have to do a play.

Kearns   Get away. Harry, they're doing a play. What is it?

Martyn   *The Wooing of Emer.*

Kearns   Ghost story, is it?

Martyn   It's about the saving of Ireland's soul.

Long pause.

Martyn   It's a comedy.

Eddie   Right so. But it says here it's a political offence.

Kearns   Dear, dear, dear.

Martyn   No no no, we were advertising our play, we got caught up in the . . .

Kearns   It wasn't political?

Martyn   No, it was social. Artistic. Foolish.

The **Constables** *confer.*

Kearns   We'll see what we can do.

Martyn   Thank you.

Eddie   Would you mind signing that?

Kearns   For you, Mr Wallace, we'll fetch the lady.

He goes to the cells.

Martyn   Are these the release forms?

Eddie   No, that's for my mother. And this one's for my fiancée.

Kearns *escorts* **Eva** *in.*

Eva   Martyn!

Martyn   Eva!

Eva   I knew you'd come.

Martyn   Are you all right?

Eva   Yes.

Martyn   I was so worried.

Eva   I considered it an honour. To know the inside of a cell and see . . .

Martyn   I know.

Eva   'The little tent of blue . . . '

Martyn *hurriedly stifles her with an embrace.*

The **Constables** *are enchanted.*

Eva   Martyn, you are so brave and true. You came to my rescue.

Martyn   Eva, I'd do anything for you.

Kearns   Harry, get out here, you're missing it.

Martyn   Eva, these nice policemen have agreed to release you.

Eva And so they should. You should be ashamed of yourselves, arresting a daughter of Erin.

Martyn Eva, just tell them it's all been a great mistake.

Eva A what?

Martyn Tell them you didn't mean it.

Eva But I did mean it.

Martyn Tell them you were pretending.

Eva And lie about my life's work?

Martyn Tell them, Eva.

Eva Never. Down with the King!

Eddie Take her down.

Eva Suffrage for all!

Martyn Eva!

Eva Don't treat me differently just because I'm a woman.

Eddie Lock her up.

They haul **Eva** *away and* **Martyn** *runs off in a panic.*

Scene Twenty-Two

Frank Frank leant his brow against the cool, damp tiles. People's feet walked over the glass skylight above him – walking over his grave. He'd had a few, but he still didn't feel calm. All he had to do was trust his plan. He had everything worked out. He felt inside his pocket for his ticket. His ticket. He staggered up the steep stairs of the Palace toilet, and made for the doors, for freedom.

Voice Here. You forgot your bag!

His bag is revealed. **Frank** *grabs it.*

Frank Frank took and held the brown leather bag with its gold embossed letters as if it were a lost child miraculously restored. He tried to thank the man, but it was all he could do to keep from throwing up.

He stumbled backwards onto the street and towards the theatre.

Exit.

Act Two

The Theatre

Scene One

Red curtains majestically swish closed. **Doherty** *parts them and steps out.*

Doherty   Doherty the box was sweeping the stage. He wasn't happy about it.

Doing the jobs I'm not supposed to be doing because themselves is too up themselves to be doing the things they're supposed . . .

He hears someone coming and steps back into the shadows.

Maggie   Maggie walked across, carrying a basket of costumes.

She puts down her basket.

There was no one around. She walked to the footlights. She looked out at the empty seats and imagined . . .

Doherty   Doherty the box stared at Maggie. She wore her bust like a sail and he wanted to set her rigging.

Sensing that she is no longer alone, **Maggie** *takes up her basket and flees in alarm to the dressing room.*

Maggie   Maggie was exhausted. But these costumes had to be cleaned and ironed and hung and . . .

She stops.

That's Frank's table. Those are his things. His make-up.

She cleaned his place up for him, he was a bit untidy.

She felt sick in her stomach again. She had to tell him. She would tell him tonight.

Enter **Jimmy**.

Jimmy   Hello, Maggie, I've been looking for you. I've something for you, Maggie.

Jimmy gently unbuttoned his coat and gave her the rose he had guarded for her all day.

It'll probably need a little water and all.

Maggie   It's beautiful.

Inside she was thinking: I'll give it to Frank.

Jimmy   Maggie, there's something I've been wanting to ask you, or not even ask, but tell you, I don't know how to say it exactly, but I've been thinking, and I think that, maybe, you and I could think about . . .

Doherty *walks in on them.*

Doherty   There's Jimmy. Isn't it well for you to be disturbing the ladies? Have you finished painting that wall?

Jimmy   No, Mr Doherty.

Doherty   And what are you doing, Maggie? Trying on the costumes?

Maggie   No, Mr Doherty.

Doherty   Are you going to get down to your shift and be trying on the dresses? I bet you were. I bet you were doing your dramatic speechifying. I've heard you. Maggie does be doing very well for herself with Mr Wallace's elocution lessons, probably thinking she'll be on the stage or something.

Maggie   Maggie was flustered. She didn't know if she was pleased or mortified.

Jimmy   Jimmy felt like he couldn't breathe, like he'd had all the air kicked out of him. His temples pounded, telling him that he didn't know Maggie, that there were more things she was keeping from him. His cheeks burned with shame and he caught sight of his face in the mirror. His eyes were dark.

Doherty Jimmy, stop admiring yourself and come up and help me paint that bloody back wall. As for herself, she'd better put that flower in a vase before she squeezes the life out of it.

Doherty *and* **Maggie** *leave in opposite directions.*

Jimmy Jimmy couldn't look at her, but as he turned to follow Mr Doherty he saw a petal fall.

He starts to sing his mournful song.

Doherty (*off*) Jimmy!

Exit **Jimmy**.

Scene Two

Foyer.

Willy Willy bounded up the steps to the theatre, pausing to read with joy the sign above the doorway: 'THE WOOING OF EMER. By William Hayes.' Correctly spelled. Nothing could stop him now. The play would go on, the theatre would be secured, and the Irish National Theatre of Ireland would finally, at long last – but before all the others – be inscribed in the annals of . . .

Where is everyone?

Doherty *opens the shutter of the box office.*

Doherty I've a bone to pick with you, Mr Hayes. Complimentary tickets . . .

Willy Mr Doherty, where is my company?

Doherty And a printer called Quinnell, and a butcher in Kingstown . . .

Willy Where are the actors?

Doherty And the Palace Bar, that's a right one.

Willy A bar?

Doherty   A public house, yes. There's fourteen people listed as being invited from the Palace Bar.

Willy   Frank.

Doherty   Not to mention the other establishments.

Willy   Other?

Doherty   There's Mulligan's and the Scotch House and – look at me list if you don't believe me.

Willy   But Willy walked past, a dull sense of foreboding clouding the air before him. He could swear the piano was playing a ghostly tune.

Doherty   And a Mr McKenzie was looking for you.

Enter **Maggie**.

Maggie   Hello, Mr Hayes.

Willy   Hmm?

Maggie   I just wanted to say I hope everything goes well tonight.

Willy   Thank you. You're very kind. Who are you?

Maggie   I'm Maggie, I've been doing the costumes.

Willy   Of course, of course, forgive me.

Maggie   I was wondering, Mr Hayes. I know you're busy and all, but would there be any chance of getting the money I'm owed on the costume for Miss St John, only I'm owed it for three weeks and . . .

Willy   I'm sorry Maggie, I'm a little distracted right now.

Exit **Willy**.

Doherty   Are you short, Maggie?

Maggie   He was looking at her chest again.

Doherty   Maybe I can give it to you from petty cash. Shall we have a poke in the little box?

Maggie   I'll pay it back.

He follows her into the box office and grabs her.

Doherty   Look in the pocket, Maggie.

Maggie   I'd rather not.

Doherty   It's in me pocket, Maggie. Take it out.

Maggie   Don't be talking to me like that.

Doherty   Now who's got air and graces? Aren't you only from Townsend Street?

They wrestle.

Enter **Jimmy**.

Jimmy   Jimmy burst in on them.

Maggie   Jimmy!

Doherty (*letting go of her*) Now, now.

Enter **Willy**, *steaming.*

Willy   What's the meaning of all this? The set isn't finished. What's going on?

Jimmy   Jimmy was shaking. Everyone having a go on Maggie but him.

Maggie   It's nothing, it's . . . nothing happened.

Exit **Maggie** *and* **Doherty**.

Jimmy   And Jimmy stormed out . . .

Jimmy *leaves as* **Trench** *enters.*

Trench   . . . Past the Man in the Trenchcoat.

Who's in charge here?

Willy   I am. Are you here about the rent?

Trench   What's your name?

Willy   I am William Hayes, Esquire, producer and manager. You see, a funny thing happened. I was on my way here with the money and . . .

Trench   And you're doing a play?

Willy   We most certainly are. And I was robbed. Robbed.

Trench   Tonight?

Willy   It is our opening.

Trench   *The Wowing of Emer.*

Willy   No, that was a misprint.

Trench   It's a funny day to be doing a play, isn't it?

Willy   Is it?

Trench   Today of all days. His Majesty honouring this city with his presence. People gathering outside. Anti-war placards, anti-government leaflets.

Willy   People?

Trench   Perhaps you're hoping for a riot.

Willy *follows* **Trench** *off.*

Scene Three

Martyn   Martyn ran to the theatre. Sweat, horses, trams (klang klang klang), he almost got killed. He got a stitch! He ran and ran.

Past the awning and down the alley to the stage door . . .

Maggie   Straight into Maggie.

Martyn   Calamity!

Maggie   Mr Wallace, you poor man, the state of you. What's happened?

Martyn   Such kindness, such sweet kindness and your eyes are so blue.

Maggie   What is it?

Martyn   We can't do the play.

And Martyn saw the topless towers of Ilium and the dark black clouds of destruction gather over Troy.

Enter **Willy**.

Willy   Not for the first time, Willy felt the Horsemen of the Apocalypse whinny on his opening.

Martyn, thank Christ you're here. Listen, you can't touch the walls or anything black. Look at my hands. Martyn, what is it?

Martyn *is gibbering.*

Willy   I'm sorry. I didn't catch that.

Martyn *gibbers some more.*

Willy   Still not with you.

Martyn   Eva's in gaol.

And the topless towers of Ilium caught fire.

Willy   The burning, lofty towers came crashing down.

Martyn   The walls of Troy were breached and tumbled down.

Willy   The battlements that had shored up a wondrous city collapsed.

Martyn   And the clouds, the black clouds of despair . . .

Maggie   . . . parted and a golden ray of hope shone down, a ladder to the stars . . .

Willy   Everywhere he looked, Willy saw smouldering corpses, the burnt and ruined walls of Troy, destruction, anarchy . . .

Martyn   What are we going to do?

Willy   I don't know.

Maggie   Mr Hayes.

Willy   We need someone.

Martyn   But who?

Maggie   Mr Hayes.

Willy   Maggie, your eyes are so blue.

Martyn   We need someone.

Willy   Someone who knows the lines. A voice.

Martyn   A voice to bring people to their knees.

Willy   And then raise them with the hope of freedom and nationhood.

Maggie   'People of Ireland . . . '

Willy   Not now, Maggie!

Maggie   'Rise. Rise and be men again. Follow me and place your faith in me, and I will deliver you.'

Willy *and* **Martyn** *are inspired.* **Maggie** *slips away to put on her costume.*

Willy   Her voice rang out with the force of truth.

Martyn   It moved like a solid thing down the corridors.

Willy   It bounced off the floor.

Martyn   The walls.

Willy   The ceiling.

Martyn   It hit the back wall of the theatre.

Willy   It destroyed the back wall of the theatre.

Martyn *and* **Willy**   It burned up the whole world.

Martyn   Maggie!

Willy   No, Martyn. Emer!

Scene Four

The curtains partially pull back to reveal the stage.

Downstage of the curtain is backstage, where loiterers can 'see' the action by looking off left. Similarly, the performers upstage of the curtain can 'see' those backstage by looking off right. To make an 'entrance', performers also follow this route; that is, they exit left, downstage of the curtain, and appear from upstage of the curtain, right.

Martyn *and* **Maggie** *play Act One, Scene One.*

Willy *watches greedily from the wings.*

Maggie   'Father, you have raised me always to speak the truth, to have no fear and look fortune both good and ill full in the face.'

Martyn   'Emer, you are the fairest daughter ever gendered by the loins of man. Lovelier than your mother, and with the misty light of grace which glimmers in your eyes.'

Maggie   'I must tell you that last night I had a dream, and in that dream I saw the man I love.'

Martyn   'Who is he, Emer, daughter most fair?'

Willy   Frank!

Maggie   'He frightened me, father, for he is a man of war.'

Martyn   'Who is he, Emer, fair daughter of my heart?'

Maggie   'He frightened me, for I saw him fall before his time.'

Martyn   'Who is he, Emer?'

Willy   *Where* is he? We shouldn't have started without him.

Maggie   'He is Cuchulain.'

Willy (*to actors*)   Do it again. Keep going.

Martyn   'Who is he, Emer? Emer, who is he?'

Maggie   'He is Cuchulain.'

Martyn   'Ah, Cuchulain. How that name speaks of
foreboding and yet of greatness. The very syllables ring out
like the horns announcing war. Cuchulain, Cuchulain, is he
here to woo my daughter?'

Willy   No.

Martyn   'Can it be that warlike son of Ulster I see who
glides towards us? I'll tell you what, Emer. Let us glide
towards him.'

Willy   Keep going. Please. Do something.

They check both wings. **Martyn** *seizes the initiative.*

Martyn (*sings*)   'When Irish eyes are smiling . . . '

Scene Five

Backstage. **Willy** *is dying.* **Frank** *bursts in.*

Frank   Am I late?

Willy   Frank! Put this on. Quick, quick.

Frank   Have you started? I can hear singing.

Willy   You're not drunk?

Frank   Of course I'm not drunk.

Willy   Thank Christ for that. It's bad enough losing one
lead without losing two of you.

Frank   Who's lost?

Willy   Eva.

Frank   Where's Eva?

Willy   In gaol.

Frank   In gaol. But who's . . . ?

Willy   Never mind, you're on.

Frank   But who's . . . ?

Exit **Frank**.

Willy   It's going marvellously. Don't touch the walls.

Scene Six

As **Martyn** *and* **Maggie** *reach the rousing finale of their song,* **Frank** *bursts onstage.*

Frank   Maggie?

Martyn   'Look who it is: Cuchulain. I, Forgal the Wily, will arise and go now to light the fires of Samhain.'

He exits bitterly.

Maggie   'I, Emer, daughter of Forgal the Wily, greet you, warrior.'

Frank *dries.*

Maggie   Have you something to say to me?

Frank   'I see a sweet country; I could rest my weapon there.'

Maggie   'No man will rest there till he has stayed awake from autumn to spring and from summer to winter.'

Frank   'I see a sweet country; I will rest my weapon there.'

Maggie   'No man will rest there till he has killed a hundred enemies of my people at every ford.'

Frank   'This I will do for you, Emer, daughter of Forgal, for you are a worthy prize.'

Maggie   'My heart rejoices, but I fear our lot together will be a bitter cup of sorrow.'

Frank   'I would drink that cup to the lees if your lips were joined to mine.'

She embraces him in delight.

Maggie   'Swear you will not forsake me. Do not ever leave my side lest terrible things befall us.'

Frank   'I freely make my oath, my pledge to you, Emer. I will ever be true to thee and never leave your side.'

End of scene. They bow. Curtains close.

Scene Seven

Backstage.

Frank   You're fantastic.

Maggie   No, you are.

Frank   Where's my bag?

He rushes off.

Martyn *and* **Willy** *trot out from the wings.*

Willy   Maggie, thank you.

Martyn   Exquisite, Maggie, your nostrils actually flared.

Maggie   Is that good?

Martyn   More than good.

Willy   And you know the lines. Well done, Frank. Frank?

Exit **Willy** *and* **Martyn** *after* **Frank**.

Maggie   I can't believe it. I'm on stage. I'm an actress. I think I'm going to be sick.

Frank *hurtles past and she grabs him.* **Jimmy** *sees this.*

Maggie   Frank. Kiss me.

Frank   Here?

Maggie   Can I see you later? I need to talk . . .

Frank   I won't be here later, Maggie.

Maggie   Why, where are you going?

Frank   I can't tell you.

She is stunned. **Willy** *enters.*

Willy   Call for Act Two. Positions everybody. Maggie.
Frank. Martyn.

People dash madly around. **Maggie** *tries to talk to* **Frank** *as . . .*

Scene Eight

Curtains open once more. The play resumes.

Frank   'Emer, I swear to you on my knees that I do not
leave you lightly.'

Pause.

'My doings will be great and spoken of among the great
doings of heroes in their strength.'

Maggie   You don't love me, do you?

Frank   'Emer, my queen, my bride, my soul, I kneel and
seek your blessing for my task.'

Maggie   It meant nothing to you. You couldn't even speak
to me for weeks. You just want me to disappear.

Frank   'I have cause, O Emer, most fair.'

Maggie   'What cause would excuse a promise made in
love?'

Frank   'The cause of Ireland.'

Maggie   What do I care about Ireland, when you treat me
like a girl from the streets?

Frank   'My vows are worthless while my people are not
free.'

Maggie   Don't leave me.

Frank   'I will prove my love and make you and my people
proud of me.'

Maggie   Promise me you won't go.

Frank   Goodbye.

Exit **Frank**.

Maggie   Frank!

In despair **Maggie** *tries to follow him.*

Martyn *deftly intercepts her and keeps the play alive.*

Martyn   'Come, Emer. Tara's Halls await your song of sorrow.'

Scene Nine

Backstage.

Frank *comes backstage, and starts handing his costume to* **Willy**.

Willy   I've never seen anything like it, it's so real. I don't care if she keeps changing the lines. I'm in love.

Frank   Will you look after Maggie?

Willy   Do you think I should pay her? Where are you going?

Frank   There's something I have to do.

Willy   What? Where? But what about your death scene?

Frank   You play the part.

Willy   I beg your pardon?

Frank   I have to play mine.

He leaves the theatre carrying his bag.

Willy   Jimmy, come here. Your country needs you.

Enter **Jimmy**.

Willy   Jimmy, you're Cuchulain, put that on you and tie yourself to the post.

Jimmy   I don't know what to say.

Willy   Don't thank me now. Remember you're Cuchulain. The battle has raged, you've fought them all, but you've lost a lot of blood and the raven of death is circling, circling, coming to land on your still warm corpse. Now go out there and die a hero's death for Ireland. And don't touch the walls.

He shoves **Jimmy** *on his way.*

Enter **Eva**.

Eva   Willy, Willy. I'm here.

Willy   Eva.

Eva   You've no idea how sorry I am. William, I almost didn't make it. Everything we've fought for, all our dreams . . . But now we can start the show.

Martyn*'s voice is heard.*

Eva   Willy? You've started?

Willy   Have we?

Eva   But how? Who is playing my . . . ?

Maggie *wails for Cuchulain.*

Eva   She? Her? The costumes? Willy, how could you? Our play.

Willy   You weren't here.

Eva   I was in gaol, Willy.

Willy   And I admire you for it, Eva.

Eva   I have to go on, Willy. Surely you understand.

Willy   I do, Eva, I do, but the thing is: she's wonderful.

Eva   I have to do the last speech.

Willy   She's amazing. She's a natural.

Eva   You're in love with her.

Willy   No, I . . .

Eva   You have sacrificed everything we've worked for, I've worked for, for a seamstress.

Willy   You don't understand, Eva. The play works with her in it.

Eva   I want to do Emer's speech. And I'm going to do it.

Willy   I won't let you.

Eva   You let me sign the lease for this theatre. Get out of my way. *Na Inghinidhe na hEireann* are waiting for me. I'm coming, sisters.

She sails on stage . . .

Scene Ten

Past him. **Jimmy** *is tied to a tree.* **Maggie** *is in shock.* **Martyn** *is in full spate.*

Martyn   'So speak, Emer, speak. Before the ruined body of Cuchulain, tied to the holy tree, where the raven on his shoulder drinks now his precious blood. O Emer, you who have our hearts have now our ears. Speak and we will . . . '

Eva *bursts on and marches to the footlights.*

Eva   'Men of Ireland, sons of Erin, your country needs you, rise. Do not listen because I am Emer.'

Maggie *is roused to disagree.*

Maggie   I am Emer.

Eva   'Do not listen because I am your queen.'

Maggie   I am.

Maggie *and* **Eva**   'Do not listen because I am the wife of Cuchulain, the great hero who is slain.'

Jimmy *dies; the crow on his shoulder gives a squawk.*

Maggie *and* **Eva**   'You must listen because I repeat only what your own hearts are telling me. We mourn, we mourn, but we must not despair. The call is noble, the time is now. Men of Ireland, sons of Erin, rise, rise.'

Martyn   Up the Republic!

Maggie *and* **Eva**   'You must do whatever it takes to resist the wrongful occupation of your land.'

There is a shuddering explosion outside. Lights flicker. Dust falls. There is the tinkle of falling glass.

Willy   Willy peered out the window on the stairs. Dust was falling gently on the rubble and the stones and a perfect unblemished young man lying peacefully on his back, staring at the sky, dead. Willy clutched his precious speech. 'Men and women of Ireland. In your name and the name of our noble . . . '

Enter **Trench**.

Trench   Ladies and gentlemen, I urge you to remain calm. In the interest of National Security we're taking control of this building.

Willy   But my speech, my play, my theatre.

Trench   I'm afraid now is not the time for that sort of thing.

He pushers them all off, **Willy** *being the last to go as he looks out despairingly at the emptying stalls. The curtains close.*

Act Three

Nighttown

Scene One

Bare stage.

Maggie Maggie was standing in the middle of the stage. The lights were going out one by one. She could hear them creaking and ticking as they cooled. And even as they were dying, a faint light seemed to hang about them as if it was afraid to leave.

Jimmy You were brilliant. In the play, I mean. You were . . . brilliant.

Maggie Was I?

Jimmy It was like you were another person.

Maggie Where is everyone?

Jimmy Talking to the police, I think. You know, Maggie, I still . . . I still have feelings for you. That is, I still think . . . I still . . .

Maggie Don't, Jimmy.

Jimmy I have to, Maggie. I have to. I love you, Maggie, more than ever.

Maggie Not after all that's happened.

Jimmy Even after you throwing me over and thinking yourself too good for the likes of me. I'd still take you back.

Maggie Don't you see, Jimmy, I could never go back. I'm in the theatre now.

Jimmy You don't think they care anything for you?

Maggie They do. They understand me.

She troops off, followed by **Jimmy**.

Scene Two

*One by one, the members of the company file on and stand in line.
They are being interrogated simultaneously by* **Trench** (*unseen*).

Willy No, William *Hayes.*

Trench (*off*) You didn't write the . . . what was it, *Countess
Cathleen?*

Willy No. Look, is this about the stolen money? I can
explain. You see . . .

Martyn I'm an actor.

Trench (*off*) And how long have you been in the
Daughters of Erin?

Eva *Inghinidhe na hEireann.* Seven years.

Trench (*off*) And the Boer War Committee?

Eva Until it's no longer needed.

Trench (*off*) *Cathleen Ni Houlihan?*

Willy No.

Maggie I used to work in a hotel.

Jimmy A carpenter.

Trench (*off*) Are you or have you ever been in the Irish
Republican Brotherhood?

Willy No.

Eva No.

Jimmy No.

Maggie No.

Martyn No, but I was in *The Corsican Brothers.*

Eva Can't you see we're busy? And surely you could be
better employed catching criminals.

Willy   No, I have never addressed the *Cumann na nGaedheal* nor have I ever been arrested.

Martyn   I don't even know anything *about* politics.

We see **Maggie**.

Trench (*off*)   You're a pretty thing.

Martyn   I'll tell you anything you want to hear.

Willy   We are theatre artists.

Eva   Don't you know who I am?

We see **Martyn**, *sobbing*.

Trench (*off*)   Get rid of him.

We see **Maggie** *once again*.

Maggie   Go to hell.

Trench *steps out into the light*.

Trench   And where is the brave Cuchulain?

Willy   The very question our play seeks to pose.

Trench   I beg your pardon?

Willy   Where are the heroic men . . .

Eva   . . . and women . . .

Willy   . . . of Ireland in this dark time of oppression and government interference?

Eva   Well done, William.

Trench   Yes, well, I want to speak to him.

Willy   I'm sorry to disappoint you, but he's a mythical figure. He doesn't actually exist. Now, if you have no further questions I will be getting back to work. Goodbye.

Trench   Perhaps I'm not making myself clear. Where is Frank?

Willy   Frank?

Jimmy   I don't know.

Maggie   I don't want to see him ever again.

Eva   I don't recognise your authority.

Martyn *weeps.*

Trench   Where is your brother?

Willy   I don't care!

Trench   You must hand him over.

Willy   Can't we talk about this tomorrow, after the play?
It's just that I have a lot of things to look after, what with
the press and recasting and . . .

Trench   The play won't be on tomorrow.

Willy   What do you mean? We're running for two weeks,
and hope to extend.

Trench   You will be receiving a letter from the Castle
informing you that His Excellency the Lord Lieutenant does
not feel that such sensitive material can be presented.

Willy   Sensitive?

Martyn   Oh but it is, William, extremely sensitive. Beautiful.

Willy   But isn't it enough that tonight is a disaster? Surely
we don't have to be ruined for the whole week?

Trench   I don't think you grasp the seriousness of the
situation. We have the King's security to consider.

Willy   But it's just a play.

Trench   Plays contain coded messages.

Willy   What if we change the title?

Trench   I beg your pardon?

Willy   Or make cuts. I mean, we weren't trying to offend
anyone. Least of all His Majesty.

Trench   A bit late for that now.

Willy   We'll have a whip-round. A benefit performance.

Trench   I don't think so.

Willy   In aid of the afflicted. Maybe His Majesty would like to come?

Trench   I don't think you understand me. Your play is finished. It is over. It is withdrawn.

Exit **Trench**.

Scene Three

Maggie   What am I going to do?

Eva   Maggie, while we all wish you well, there are others more unfortunate than yourself.

She rolls up her sleeves and prepares to go outside.

Come on, everyone. It's time to show our mettle. There are people out there who need us.

Willy   Eva, you're right. People are depending on us. Martyn, how quickly could we scrub up something from our repertoire? We don't want to annoy them, so I'm thinking something light, a little West Endy, a little farcey. Something like . . .

Martyn   *His Hairy Legs*.

Willy   I mean, they can't possibly object to that.

Martyn   And we could do the scene where I dress up as my own mother.

Willy   By God, they'll have to try harder than that if they think they can stop us. We're theatre people! We must stick together! The show must go on!

Eva   William, I never thought I'd say this, but I am ashamed.

Willy   Never mind, Eva, you did your best.

Eva   I'm ashamed at you.

Willy   Me?

Eva   I thought you believed in our cause, and here you are ready to sacrifice your principles for the first policeman who comes knocking.

Willy   What are you talking about? I'm trying to save our company.

Maggie   Mr Hayes? If she doesn't want to be in it . . .

Willy   Not now, Emer.

Eva   Emer?

She storms off.

Willy   Eva? Come back. I'm sorry, it was a misprint.

He follows her off. The others look at each other. **Willy** *and* **Eva** *are heard arguing before they stomp back on.*

Eva   We're not doing any more plays, Willy. It's not right. Not in the face of suffering.

Willy   What do you know about suffering? You've never had to haggle and scrounge. You've never had to sacrifice anything. You've never wanted for anything in your whole life.

Eva   William!

Willy   This isn't a platform for your social profile, your meetings and your *cumanna* and your committees. This is the noble call. A chance to make our mark on history. Our chance to create a National Drama to be proud of.

Eva   *His Hairy Legs?*

Willy   It's not about the plays, it's about the building. As long as we have the building it is our duty to use it, to act for our country. We can't give in now. What time is it? Maybe we can still make the morning papers. We must announce the survival of the National Theatre in the face of temporary crisis. You don't have the time? (*Patting his* *pockets.*) Do you think it's after eleven? Doesn't anybody have the time? What are you doing with that lease?

Eva *holds the document at arm's length.*

Eva   I thought we were partners, but I see you value my contribution not at all.

Willy   What are you talking about, Eva?

Eva   Where's the watch I gave you? Where is it?

Willy   I don't have it any more.

Eva   Where is it?

Willy   I have it in a safe place. It was stolen. I was mugged. Don't tear that lease, Eva. Eva, listen to me, I was over-excited and over-emotional. I didn't mean what I said.

Eva   It seems you never do.

Willy   Don't do it, Eva.

Eva   I don't believe you any more.

Willy   I'm sorry about the watch. But it's just a watch, Eva. That, however is . . .

Eva   It wasn't just a watch. It was the symbol of our partnership, the token of our bond, the proof of our love.

And Eva tore the lease. And tore it again. And again. And again.

The pieces flew . . .

Willy   . . . into the air in a brief white flurry and fell silently around them, a snowfall of loss and recrimination.

Clutching a scrap of paper, he falls to his knees and lets out a sob.

My National Theatre!

Eva   Look at you, William. Look at what you've become. You have lost your soul. (*She draws herself up.*) Who's coming with me in my mission to help the afflicted?

Nobody does.

Eva   Theatre of the people? Bunch of fairweathers.

Exit **Eva**.

Maggie   Mr Hayes? Mr Wallace?

Jimmy *tries to take her arm. She bats him off indignantly and storms out.* **Jimmy** *follows her, as always.*

Martyn   Perhaps we can tour?

Willy *gives him a hollow look and* **Martyn** *slopes sadly away.*

Willy   What have I done to deserve this? How much lower can a man fall?

Castle Agent (*off*)   You're under arrest.

Willy   What?

Castle Agent (*off*)   Take him away.

Willy   But I didn't do anything. I'm not a republican. I'm not even a nationalist. I couldn't care less about this stupid country.

Castle Agent   We found your bag.

Willy   My Gladstone? Where are you taking me? Unhand me!

He is violently removed.

Scene Four

Theatre dressing room.

Maggie   Maggie stormed into the dressing room for the last time.

All Frank's little things stared up at her. His make-up. His stupid rose.

She snaps it in two and pricks herself on a thorn. In a rage she shoves everything off the table.

She grabbed a shirt of Frank's and tore it . . .

And then she saw the ticket.

It had fallen on the floor beside Frank's things. A ticket. For the ferry to Liverpool. Leaving tonight. Midnight.

Oh my God. That's why he left.

She looks around to see if anyone is watching her.

Why didn't he ask her to come with him?

Enter **Jimmy**.

Jimmy   Where are you going, Maggie?

Maggie   Leave me alone, Jimmy. I don't want you, I can't stand you.

Jimmy   They don't want you, Maggie. You're coming home with me.

Maggie   Let go of my arm, you're hurting me.

Jimmy   You're coming home to Townsend Street, where you belong.

Maggie   I love Frank. I'm having his baby.

Jimmy   Oh my God, Maggie.

She waves the ticket in his face.

Maggie   Look. We're running away together. I'm leaving on the last boat tonight. He's waiting for me right now.

She leaves triumphantly. **Jimmy** *looks after her, before decisively heading off in the opposite direction.*

Scene Five

Street.

Eva   For bandages, Eva had torn up whatever costumes she could lay her hands on, and had requisitioned curtains to make stretchers.

You, what do you think you're doing? Carry him properly.

She had divided over-curious bystanders and her Daughters
of Erin into teams to ferry the wounded to the Jervis Street
Hospital.

That's not how you tie a tourniquet. For God's sake,
woman, it's only blood.

Exit.

Scene Six

Jammet's Restaurant.

Martyn   Mr Hayes and Miss St John will be joining me in
a smidgin. Something to drink? I mustn't. Maybe a small
one.

Martyn stood at the bar in Jammet's, waiting for a table to
be cleared. He was too long in the game to let a first-night
disaster get him down. There was a decorum to be observed
in such matters. One had to preserve an equanimous façade.

Waiter!

Scene Seven

Willy *is hauled to the city morgue.*

Willy   Willy was hauled briskly over the shallow puddles
and cobbles . . .

What do you mean, you've found him? Where are you
taking me?

. . . to the forbidding squat square building at the corner of
Marlborough and Abbey Streets where, he was plunged
down the steps into the main room of the morgue.

The silence was insistent. A body lay on a marble-topped
table, covered by a dirty sheet.

From the dark comes a voice.

Castle Agent (*off*)   Is that Cuchulain?

Willy   Oh no.

Willy stood before the covered body, the wet soles of his boots leaking water on the floor.

Frank?

The morgue assistant picked up the corners of the dirty sheet.

To reveal the body of . . .

A young man. His face was grey and curiously unmarked by the blast. It was the dead boy he'd seen near the theatre.

Oh my God. Frank, what have you done?

Castle Agent (*off*)   He's admitting it.

Willy   You idiot. This isn't what we were fighting for.

Castle Agent (*off*)   Fighting for. Get that down.

Willy   When I said we were to act for Ireland I meant *act* for Ireland, not this. Not kill people. Frank, my own brother, a murderer.

Castle Agent (*off*)   All right, sign here.

Willy   What?

Castle Agent (*off*)   That's your statement. Sign here. And we need you to identify the body.

Willy   What am I signing?

Castle Agent (*off*)   Your sworn statement accusing your brother of tonight's terrible crime.

Willy   Accusing him?

Castle Agent (*off*)   Well if he wasn't dead, he'd swing tomorrow morning. Now, for form's sake, is this the body of Frank Hayes? You can't protect him any more.

Willy   Willy didn't know where the voice came from, but he turned slowly to the morgue assistant and the plain clothes detective and cleared his throat.

That's him. That's my brother. God have mercy on his soul.

A sob burst from his lungs. The hot unbidden tears of grief coursed down his cheek. He was truly mourning his brother, his only brother. Dead, dead. What an idea for a play!

And Willy came up short as he stepped into the light rain outside the morgue. If that wasn't Frank, Frank was out there, somewhere, alone, possibly hurt, in danger. What was he doing? Where was he now?

Exit **Willy**, *shadowed by a* **Castle Agent**.

Scene Eight

Frank *is riding a whore.*

Frank   Frank was sweating and had begun to shake. Perhaps he'd caught a chill from the rain, or perhaps it was the whiskey.

But he kept at it. Anything to keep his mind off . . . off . . . off . . .

He was a wanted man. Possibly the most wanted man in Ireland. The police, the British, the IRB, they all wanted him dead.

Whore 1   Are you enjoying yourself?

Frank *bursts into tears and staggers for the door.*

Whore 1   Hey, where's my money?

Frank *searches his pockets in a mounting panic.*

Frank   Where's my . . . Where's my ticket? Oh God.

He runs off.

Whore 1   Hey! Stop him. Thief!

She pursues him.

Scene Nine

Bride Street.

Jimmy   Jimmy passed down the dark alleys, past the drunks and the sick.

To a small room above a pub in Bride Street.

He pushes in the door and enters.

I know where he is.

The pub goes quiet.

His throat was tight, he couldn't swallow.

Maloney (*off*)   Where is he, Jimmy?

Jimmy   The North Wall. Last boat.

Maloney (*off*)   You sure you heard right?

Jimmy   I heard it all right. Didn't she tell me right to my face?

Maloney (*off*)   Right, lads.

Jimmy   But you must promise not to hurt her.

He is thrown out onto the street.

The rain began to fall. Jimmy thought of the rose.

Scene Ten

Tyrone Street. Several **Whores** *emerge from the darkness.*

Willy   Willy turned down Tyrone Street.

Whore 1   Are you looking for company?

Willy   No thank you.

Whore 2   Maybe you prefer me, sir?

Whore 3   Or me, a redhead?

Whore 2   See my petticoats?

Whore 1   Like a dance?

Whore 3   I've a room.

Willy   Her breath was a solid. It hit him between the eyes, a methylated fist. Her skin was white. His head began to turn.

They strip him of his hat, his jacket and tie.

Whore 2   Are you going to play with us?

Willy   Please, don't touch me. Leave me alone.

Whore 3   What's wrong? Have you lost your bottle?

Whore 1   He's lost his bottle.

Willy   I've not lost my bottle. My bottle is . . .

Whore 1   Go back home to England.

Whore 3   You big Brit ponce.

Willy   How dare you. This is my home.

Whore 2   Go on, you fat foreign lump.

Willy   This is my country and I would –

*As they leave, one of the **Whores** hits him from behind with a bottle.* **Willy** *staggers off, concussed.*

Scene Eleven

Railway Arches.

Maggie   As she passed under the railway arches, Maggie breathed the sweet rank smell of alcohol that seemed to swim out from the warehouses. She held her collar closed against the rain.

Now Frank was her only hope. If she stayed here without him, she'd end up in the Laundry or somewhere in disgrace.

Once she told him, he'd be bound to take her with him. She was going to leave for good. The tenements, the slaving, and her ma and her brothers as well. If she could spare it she'd send over something for the rent. She really would.

And sure, once she got married, she'd be able to come home and show them the baby. But how was she going to find Frank? The ticket said the North Wall, but where exactly? Was there a waiting place for those who were running away?

Voice   Come back here, you little slut.

Exit **Maggie**.

Scene Twelve

Bridge.

Eva   Eva was wet and tired and now she had to walk home. She had to cross the river which was down this little alley . . .

Voice 1   Are you in business?

Eva   The voices pawed her and snatched at her clothes.

Leave me alone. I'm trying to help you people!

Voice 2   Come over here and help me, then!

Voice 1   I'll help meself!

Eva   Through the gloom she saw the skeleton of the Halfpenny Bridge. The stink of the river rose above the stench of the slum. The black waters of the Liffey washing out to sea all the misery and hope. She was almost there.

Voice 2   Come back here when I'm talking to you.

Eva   Let go of me, you dirty, dirty filth!

Scene Thirteen

Jammet's.

Martyn   We must hellenise this pitiful island. Rouse yourselves, you inverted Jesuits, from out your Firbolg melancholy to Attic joy −

He vomits onto himself.

Actually. I think that wine was corked. My bill? Send it to the National Theatre.

He is thrown out onto the street.

Philistines!

Martyn couldn't see clearly before him. It was like there was a mist before his eyes . . . It was raining! Rain!

And he walked slap bang into a Dublin Metropolitan Policeman.

Thank God you're here. I'm turning myself in. Wait, where are you going? Aren't you going to arrest me? I'm Martyn Wallace. Fenian rebel and Vice-President of the Irish National Theatre of Ireland. I need to go to gaol. Please. I've nowhere else to go!

He stumbles and falls.

Scene Fourteen

Willy *staggers on, feeling the back of his head. He approaches a drunken* **Mendicant**.

Willy   Where . . . Where . . . Where am I?

Mendicant   Here.

Willy   I thought I was somewhere else.

Mendicant   One of those days.

The **Mendicant** *hands him a bottle of whiskey.*

Willy   I saw a dead boy today.

Mendicant   Anyone you knew?

Willy   No. I thought it was my brother.

Swig.

Mendicant   I've a family like that.

Willy   He's dead. He'll never taste the joys of . . . you know, all this.

He throws up.

Mendicant   Didn't eat?

Willy   Why did he die?

Mendicant   Fever, was it? Consumption? He was hit by a tram?

Willy   For Ireland.

Mendicant   Ah, Jesus. Give us that. For Ireland. Fair play.

The **Mendicant** *finds the bottle is empty.*

Willy   I mean, for us. He was killed in our name.

Mendicant   I never killed anybody. But I'd murder another drink.

Willy   His blood is on our hands . . . Frank.

Mendicant   Gerry.

Willy   What have you done? What have I done?

Mendicant   What have you done?

Willy   I urged him on. I told him to sacrifice everything for Ireland. But it's I who have sacrificed everything. It's true. I have lost my soul.

Mendicant   Wait, are you from the Salvation Army?

Willy   I have to save him. I have to save my brother.

Mendicant   I knew it.

Exit **Mendicant**.

Willy   Frank? Frank?

Exit **Willy**.

Scene Fifteen

The North Wall.

Frank   Frank stumbled along, hugging the walls, the shadows. He felt sick. How could he have lost his ticket? He had to get out, he had to escape.

He reached the quays and turned left. The ferry! Its black mass was silhouetted against the night, lights from the portholes winked in the gathering mist.

The ship's horn bells out in the fog.

It was so close. He heard footsteps. Was somebody following him?

Frank *hides to one side.*

Two **IRB Men** *swagger on, looking for* **Frank**.

Boylan   They've started boarding the ship.

Maloney   There's too many soldiers.

Exit **IRB Men**.

Frank   Frank was sweating and shivering in the cold night air. A mist was beginning to roll off the dark river. He heard footsteps, boots, cries and moans. He saw . . .

Maggie *walks on.*

Frank   Maggie?

Maggie   Frank? Is it you?

Frank   Maggie, what are you doing here?

Maggie   I found the ticket.

Frank   You found it? Thank God.

Willy *passes by in the night, but doesn't see them.*

Willy   Frank? Frank?

Exit **Willy**.

Frank   You're having a baby?

Maggie   I wanted to tell you, but there wasn't time.

Frank   A little baby.

The ship's horn sounds again.

Frank   Maggie, I have to go. Give me the ticket.

Maggie   Don't you have one already?

Frank   No, you've got it. You said you had it. That's the ticket.

Maggie   What about my ticket?

Frank   You don't have one. Go home.

Maggie   I can't. What will I do without you?

Frank *sees the* **IRB Men**.

Frank   Oh Jesus. They're after me. Give me the ticket.

Maggie   You can't leave me, Frank.

Frank   Do you want me killed? Give it to me!

The **IRB Men** *are getting closer.*

Frank *wrestles with* **Maggie** *for the ticket and runs off.*

Willy *appears.*

Maggie   Frank!

Willy   Frank?

He runs towards her as **Maggie** *chases after her lover.*

The **IRB Men** *grab him.*

Maloney   We've been looking for you.

Willy   What have you done with my –

They punch **Willy** *and start marching him off.*

Willy   Let go of me.

British Soldier (*off*)   Halt. Put your hands in the air.

Boylan   Quick.

Maloney   It's the Brits.

The **IRB Men** *scatter, leaving* **Willy** *to fend for himself.*

British Soldier (*off*)   Stay where you are or we'll open –

A shot rings out.

Willy   Don't shoot.

British Soldier (*off*)   Shut yer hole, Fenian scum. You're under arrest.

Willy   You don't understand, I'm not actually with them. You see, this has all been a mistake. It's all been a terrible –

Willy *is shot suddenly, violently, stone dead.*

Scene Sixteen

Maggie   No! Frank!

Maggie stood by the railings. There was shouting and policemen. A surge of people round her. Maggie's head was swimming. She heard cattle moaning from their pens. They'd all left her. She was on her own now. On her own.

And inside her a new life was beating out its pitiful existence.

What future had she, had any of them, in this dark place?

Ship's horn.

The ship's siren sounded out a long, painful cry.

She stepped back from the rush, into the shadows, the better to think.

The darkness swallowed her up.

Methuen Modern Plays

include work by

Edward Albee
Jean Anouilh
John Arden
Margaretta D'Arcy
Peter Barnes
Sebastian Barry
Brendan Behan
Dermot Bolger
Edward Bond
Bertolt Brecht
Howard Brenton
Anthony Burgess
Simon Burke
Jim Cartwright
Caryl Churchill
Noël Coward
Lucinda Coxon
Sarah Daniels
Nick Darke
Nick Dear
Shelagh Delaney
David Edgar
David Eldridge
Dario Fo
Michael Frayn
John Godber
Paul Godfrey
David Greig
John Guare
Peter Handke
David Harrower
Jonathan Harvey
Iain Heggie
Declan Hughes
Terry Johnson
Sarah Kane
Charlotte Keatley
Barrie Keeffe
Howard Korder

Robert Lepage
Doug Lucie
Martin McDonagh
John McGrath
Terrence McNally
David Mamet
Patrick Marber
Arthur Miller
Mtwa, Ngema & Simon
Tom Murphy
Phyllis Nagy
Peter Nichols
Sean O'Brien
Joseph O'Connor
Joe Orton
Louise Page
Joe Penhall
Luigi Pirandello
Stephen Poliakoff
Franca Rame
Mark Ravenhill
Philip Ridley
Reginald Rose
Willy Russell
Jean-Paul Sartre
Sam Shepard
Wole Soyinka
Shelagh Stephenson
Peter Straughan
C. P. Taylor
Theatre de Complicite
Theatre Workshop
Sue Townsend
Judy Upton
Timberlake Wertenbaker
Roy Williams
Snoo Wilson
Victoria Wood

Methuen Contemporary Dramatists

include

John Arden (two volumes)
Arden & D'Arcy
Peter Barnes (three volumes)
Sebastian Barry
Dermot Bolger
Edward Bond (six volumes)
Howard Brenton
   (two volumes)
Richard Cameron
Jim Cartwright
Caryl Churchill (two volumes)
Sarah Daniels (two volumes)
Nick Darke
David Edgar (three volumes)
Ben Elton
Dario Fo (two volumes)
Michael Frayn (three volumes)
David Greig
John Godber (two volumes)
Paul Godfrey
John Guare
Lee Hall (two volumes)
Peter Handke
Jonathan Harvey
   (two volumes)
Declan Hughes
Terry Johnson
   (two volumes)
Sarah Kane
Barrie Keefe
Bernard-Marie Koltès
David Lan
Bryony Lavery
Deborah Levy
Doug Lucie

David Mamet (four volumes)
Martin McDonagh
Duncan McLean
Anthony Minghella
   (two volumes)
Tom Murphy (four volumes)
Phyllis Nagy
Anthony Neilsen
Philip Osment
Louise Page
Stewart Parker (two volumes)
Joe Penhall
Stephen Poliakoff
   (three volumes)
David Rabe
Mark Ravenhill
Christina Reid
Philip Ridley
Willy Russell
Eric-Emmanuel Schmitt
Ntozake Shange
Sam Shepard (two volumes)
Shelagh Stephenson
Wole Soyinka (two volumes)
David Storey (three volumes)
Sue Townsend
Judy Upton
Michel Vinaver
   (two volumes)
Arnold Wesker (two volumes)
Michael Wilcox
Roy Williams
Snoo Wilson (two volumes)
David Wood (two volumes)
Victoria Wood

Methuen World Classics

include

Jean Anouilh (two volumes)
Brendan Behan
Aphra Behn
Bertolt Brecht (eight volumes)
Büchner
Bulgakov
Calderón
Čapek
Anton Chekhov
Noël Coward (eight volumes)
Feydeau
Eduardo De Filippo
Max Frisch
John Galsworthy
Gogol
Gorky (two volumes)
Harley Granville Barker
  (two volumes)
Victor Hugo
Henrik Ibsen (six volumes)
Jarry

Lorca (three volumes)
Marivaux
Mustapha Matura
David Mercer (two volumes)
Arthur Miller (five volumes)
Molière
Musset
Peter Nichols (two volumes)
Joe Orton
A. W. Pinero
Luigi Pirandello
Terence Rattigan
  (two volumes)
W. Somerset Maugham
  (two volumes)
August Strindberg
  (three volumes)
J. M. Synge
Ramón del Valle-Inclán
Frank Wedekind
Oscar Wilde

Methuen Classical Greek Dramatists

Aeschylus Plays: One
(Persians, Seven Against Thebes, Suppliants,
Prometheus Bound)

Aeschylus Plays: Two
(Oresteia: Agamemnon, Libation-Bearers, Eumenides)

Aristophanes Plays: One
(Acharnians, Knights, Peace, Lysistrata)

Aristophanes Plays: Two
(Wasps, Clouds, Birds, Festival Time, Frogs)

Aristophanes & Menander: New Comedy
(Women in Power, Wealth, The Malcontent,
The Woman from Samos)

Euripides Plays: One
(Medea, The Phoenician Women, Bacchae)

Euripides Plays: Two
(Hecuba, The Women of Troy, Iphigeneia at Aulis,
Cyclops)

Euripides Plays: Three
(Alkestis, Helen, Ion)

Euripides Plays: Four
(Elektra, Orestes, Iphigenia in Tauris)

Euripides Plays: Five
(Andromache, Herakles' Children, Herakles)

Euripides Plays: Six
(Hippolytos, Suppliants, Rhesos)

Sophocles Plays: One
(Oedipus the King, Oedipus at Colonus, Antigone)

Sophocles Plays: Two
(Ajax, Women of Trachis, Electra, Philoctetes)